Criminal Justice

Recent Scholarship

Edited by
Marilyn McShane and Frank P. Williams III

A Series from LFB Scholarly

Inside Looking Out
Jailed Fathers' Perceptions about Separation from Their Children

Jamie S. Martin

LFB Scholarly Publishing LLC
New York 2001

Library of Congress Cataloging-in-Publication Data

Martin, Jamie S.
  Inside looking out : jailed fathers' perceptions about
separation from their children / Jamie S. Martin.
     p. cm. -- (Criminal justice recent scholarship)
  Includes bibliographical references and index.
  ISBN 1-931202-18-4
  1. Prisoners--United States--Family relationships. 2. Father
and child--United States. 3. Children of prisoners--United
States. 4. Imprisonment--United States. I. Title. II. Series.
  HV8886.U5 M365 2001
  306.874'2'086920973--dc21

2001002462

ISBN 1-931202-18-4

Printed on acid-free 250-year-life paper.

Manufactured in the United States of America.

Dedication

This study is dedicated to the memory of my father, James Flick
who convinced me that I could succeed,
and in honor of my mother, Joanne Flick,
who provided the support to let me try.

Table of Contents

List of Tables and Figures

Acknowledgements

There are many individuals who contributed to the completion of this project and to whom I am grateful. First and foremost, I would like to express my love and gratitude to my biggest supporter, my husband Randy, who provided the emotional support, editing expertise, and encouragement to allow me to finish. I also want to thank my sons, Tyler and Lane, for enduring my moods and for giving me a reason to smile at the end of some very long days.

I would like to thank my colleagues Rosemary Gido, Nanci Wilson, Jake Gibbs and Dennis Giever for reading multiple drafts and providing feedback, statistical expertise and encouragement during the course of this project. I am indebted to my mentor, Kate Hanrahan, who has influenced me more than any other educator I have encountered. Thank you for making graduate education both compassionate and challenging, and thank you for the time, energy, and wisdom that you have given to me during the course of this project. Without your guidance and encouragement, this project would never have come to fruition.

I am grateful to the wardens who provided me access to their jails and all of the jail administrators and correctional officers who assisted during the data collection. I want to especially thank the fathers who participated in this research project for sharing their stories with me.

Finally, I want to thank my "family of origin" for providing me the impetus for this project. I am grateful to my parents for being wonderful role models and for their unwavering support, and to my siblings, Barb, Sharon, Cindy, Tom and Ryan, for their encouragement and for repeatedly asking, "Have you finished?" This provided me the perseverance to continue when I wanted to quit.

Introduction

The current study is the result of a question posed nearly 7 years ago in conversation with colleagues and my mentor. As we spoke about the plight of incarcerated mothers in this nation, I asked, "What about incarcerated fathers?" At the time, I was certain that there must be a good deal written on the topic, considering the sheer number of men that we incarcerate, over 1.7 million according to recent statistics (Beck, 2000). Remarkably, there was very little information available. Incarcerated fathers represent a very large and a very understudied group. Indeed, there are no accurate counts on the number of fathers who are incarcerated in our nation's jails nor on the number of children they have. An important question would seem to be why incarcerated fathers have been neglected in research.

In our culture, the mother has long been considered the most important individual in a child's life. As the primary child-rearing parent, she is responsible for "shaping" her children. Mothers are the necessary parents. Fathers have traditionally been allocated a supporting role in this process, and, it may be argued, are viewed by some as dispensable. The focus on the critical role the mother plays in her child's development has a long history. Indeed, John Bowlby, (1952) a psychoanalyst and leading expert on attachment argued that the mother-child relationship was the most important relationship during the child's formative years. Fathers were seen as necessary only

1

to the extent that they supported the mother, permitting her to more effectively care and nurture their child.

More recently, researchers have begun to reexamine the role that the father plays in the family. It is becoming clear that the once dominant view that fathers fulfill a secondary or insignificant role is not accurate. That the father plays an important role in the development and prosperity of his children is becoming increasingly evident (see for example, Lamb, 1981; Bronstein and Cowan, 1988; Marsiglio, 1995). It is also evident that a large number of children in the United States have lost their fathers to our nation's jails and prisons.

"Since 1980, the United States has engaged in the largest and most frenetic correctional buildup of any country in the history of the world" (Donzinger, 1996, p. 31). The United States has the highest incarceration rate of any industrialized nation in the world. In 1992, the incarceration rate in the United States was 455 inmates per 100,000. South Africa was second highest with 311 inmates per 100,000. In raw numbers, this translated to a total of 855,958 inmates in state and federal prisons nationwide by mid-1992 (Americans Behind Bars, 1993).

By midyear 1999, this figure had risen to an astounding 1,254,577. Of this total, 93.5% (1,173,029) were men and 6.5% (81,548) were women. In addition, there were 605,943 individuals incarcerated in our nation's jails at midyear 1999. A total of 88.8% (538,077) of the jail inmates were men and 11.2% (67,866) were women (Beck, 2000). In sum, there are approximately 1.86 million individuals behind bars in federal and state prisons and local jails and millions of individuals cycling through our nation's jails annually. The vast majority of incarcerated individuals are men, and a large proportion of these men are fathers (Mumola, 2000). Hence, a very large group of men will continue to experience this form of episodic separation from their families, and their families will experience the loss of a father or husband.

Because of the public's attitudes about crime, and our politicians' promises to "get tough," it is expected that the number of individuals incarcerated in this country will continue to increase, as will the number of individuals coming into contact with local jails. Consequently, the number of families that experience the loss of a member to the Criminal Justice System will also continue to increase, and in most instances the member lost will be a father.

The purpose of the present study is to explore and describe the meaning and significance of the paternal role to jailed fathers, and how the experience of being jailed affects that role. Being incarcerated is an especially stressful event. Individuals are removed from their homes and communities and remanded to an environment that strips them of their freedom and, while incarcerated, their identities as husbands, sons, brothers, and fathers. The stress of this experience is amplified when an individual enters a jail. Jails are often the "gateway into confinement" for all individuals. Whereas most prisons receive inmates who have already been detained for a period of time and have been through a classification process, jails receive individuals who, up until the moment they step through the door, have been living in the relative freedom of society. Consequently, being jailed is a very chaotic, disorienting experience and the stress is much more acute than that experienced in the process of being imprisoned (Gibbs, 1992).

This study examines the relationship between these two experiences – (1) fatherhood and (2) the stress of being jailed. When individuals experience stress, they often turn to family members for assistance and support. When an individual is incarcerated, however, contact with family is not readily available. Consequently, separation from loved ones results in added stress for some jailed fathers. This study sought to understand if the men's roles as fathers provided a buffer to the stress of incarceration, or conversely, if this role exacerbated the amount of stress experienced, or both. As anticipated, the father's pre-incarceration role in the family did influence his incarceration experience. Hence, the overarching questions that this study will address are:

(1) What were the experiences of the jailed fathers in their families of origin and how did these experiences influence the adult experiences of the jailed fathers?

(2) What are the characteristics of the pre-incarceration relationships of jailed fathers in their families, and do these characteristics differentially affect the stress of incarceration?

(3) What is the nature and significance of contact with family during incarceration?

(4) Do the pre-incarceration relationships of jailed fathers impact the stress of incarceration?

(5) What are the jailed fathers' plans and expectations regarding their paternal role following release?

The study falls largely in the qualitative tradition and is for the most part inductive. One of the main goals was to yield "thick description" of the perceptions of the jailed fathers. Data collection was guided by the available literature in three broad areas; (1) incarceration, jail and jail stress, (2) parenting – particularly attachment theory because of what it suggests about contact and separation, and (3) prison-based studies of incarcerated fathers.

The study is exploratory and descriptive and was conducted in two phases and at two sites. The first phase consisted of the group administration of a survey to fathers housed in two Western Pennsylvania jails. The questionnaire data provides both demographic information, and a sketch of the family, social, and pre-incarceration characteristics of the jailed fathers. The questionnaire provides information on the amount and kind of contact between jailed fathers and their family, as well. In addition, the inmates were administered a modified version of the Jail Preference Inventory and the Environmental Quality Scale to assess the level of stress caused by the jail environment. This allowed for an assessment of the sources of stress for jailed fathers, e.g. environmental causes (jail environment) versus separation from loved ones.

The second phase of the project consisted of follow-up interviews with a smaller group of fathers. These interviews provided the data directly relevant to attachment theory and the effects of enforced separation. The interviews provide a fuller understanding of the pre-incarceration roles that the men fulfilled in their families and how their families of origin influenced these roles. The interviews also provide a glimpse into how the jailed fathers are impacted by incarceration, with emphasis being given to their roles as fathers. Finally, the interviews permitted exploration of the fathers' plans and expectations following their release.

This project provides an overview of the jailed fathers in their family of origin. Special emphasis was placed on examining the father-child relationships that existed between the respondents and their fathers. A "paternal typology" was developed to describe these relationships.

Additionally, this project provides information on the pre-incarceration relationships between the jailed fathers and their children. It became clear that there were great differences between the respondents who lived with their children prior to incarceration and those who did not.

This work provides an initial glimpse at a very large and heretofore invisible group of men - jailed fathers. Jails are one of the most understudied of all correctional facilities, and fathers are probably the most understudied group in these facilities. This study begins to illuminate the effects of "doing time" on the father's role. As such, it adds to the literature in the field of corrections, specifically, to the larger discipline of criminology, and also has broader implications for attachment theory. In addition, insights were gained concerning the links between various aspects of fatherhood and the stress of incarceration.

The policy and programmatic interventions suggested by the data include providing parenting classes. Jail time is relatively short yet there are very few programming options. As a result, this environment is conducive to intervention kinds of programs, and improving the parenting skills of jailed fathers could result in positive outcomes for their children.

If attachment theory is correct – that we learn how to be a parent from our parents – it seems critical to recognize the potential damage that our policies are doing, and explore ways to insulate future generations from this damage. This may represent a significant step in helping to break the cycle of incarceration.

CHAPTER 1
Literature Review

INCARCERATED PARENTS AND THEIR CHILDREN

While our correctional facilities continue to expand at alarming rates, our understanding of the impact of incarceration has not. Societal attitudes toward prisons, jails, and inmates are predominantly negative. Many individuals believe that inmates "deserve to be locked up" and even that their families are somehow culpable (Sturges, 1998). Typically, once an individual is incarcerated, society forgets about him or her. These attitudes seem to be reflected in the academic arena, as well. While criminological research may be interested in how and why individuals "end up" in prison, and may examine the conditions that exist within institutions, with a few notable exceptions (see e.g. Toch, 1992), criminologists seem to be less concerned about the impact that incarceration has on the inmate, and downright indifferent to the impact on the family.

What most people fail to see is that "human agency or action is not only individual; it is also, unavoidably, familial, societal and institutional...All human action (even the act of a single individual) is relational" (Gilligan, 1996, p.7). Consequently, the response (punishment) is also relational, and affects the individual as well as his or her family (Carlson and Cervera, 1992).

The effect of incarceration on the family unit can be devastating. Separation from a child, spouse, or parent is always difficult to endure. The "deviant" individuals, as well as their family members, must face the prospect of long-term separation from one another and the decay of relationships that results. It is important to establish that incarceration carries with it a stigma that other forms of separation do not (Goffman, 1961). Family separation due to death or other similar causes "provides a focal concern around which the remaining members can rally and mitigate the impact of their loss. Loss of a family member due to imprisonment, on the other hand, rarely elicits a sympathetic response from significant others nor is it the kind of crisis that serves to draw members of the immediate family closer together" (Fritsch and Burkhead, 1981, p. 84). As a result, the family must endure the separation and the hardships this brings, as well as the shame of the sanction. It is imperative to recognize that this is a reality confronting a large segment of our population.

According to a recent national survey, state and federal prisons held an estimated 721,500 parents of 1,498,800 minor children. The overwhelming majority (93%) of these parents are fathers, and these fathers had an estimated 1,372,200 minor children (Mumola, 2000). It is important to note that this survey did not include information on jailed fathers and their children and if they were included these figures would be much greater. Consequently, as a discipline we have virtually ignored a very large group of parents and children who suffer from our criminal justice policies.

FRAMEWORK FOR PRESENT STUDY

By their very nature, correctional institutions contain a "captive" group and these institutions and groups have been the focus of frequent criminological inquiry. As a result, there exists a large literature base that focuses on prisons, and to a far lesser extent, jails, in the United States. Much of this literature examines the development of jails and prisons in the United States. This literature could be labeled "textbook", and consists primarily of the historical and philosophical development of our correctional institutions, their architecture, and the future of these institutions (Pollock, 1997).

There is a substantial literature base on legal issues, such as constitutional rights of prisoners (Palmer, 1985) and the death penalty (Bohm, 1991; Johnson, 1998). Within this large body of research, there is a smaller portion of research that has examined the stress of imprisonment and the adjustment of inmates to their environments and to incarceration (Toch, 1992; Gibbs, 1992; Gibbs, 1991) and the role that the family plays in this adjustment (Cobean and Power, 1978).

Within the literature that examines the stress of imprisonment, a number of studies have focused on inmate parents and the stress of being separated from one's children. Most of the research conducted in this area seems to be guided by our society's belief that mothers are the important and necessary parents. As a result, the majority of these studies have focused on incarcerated mothers (Dalley, 1997; Bloom, 1995; Johnston, 1995; Bloom and Stinehart, 1993; Pollock-Byrne, 1992; Hale, 1987; Baunach, 1985; Koban, 1983) or have examined the impact of maternal incarceration on her children (Kampfer, 1995; Hale, 1987; Henriques, 1982; McGowan and Blumenthal, 1978).

Some researches have also examined the effect of incarceration on the families of inmates, focusing on the wives (Fishman, 1990; Morris, 1965; Bakker, Janus, and Morris, 1978) and children (Gabel and Johnston, 1995; Bakker et al, 1978; Morris, 1965; Friedman and Esselystyn, 1965) of inmates. Some of these studies have suggested that the maintenance of strong family ties during imprisonment results in a more successful societal reintegration by the inmate upon release and reduced recidivism long-term (Holt and Miller, as cited in Bakker et al., 1978).

In sum, there is a rich history of research that examines prisons and prisoners, but only a small segment of that research has examined the impact of incarceration on both prisoners and their nuclear family members. This is especially true of incarcerated fathers. Only recently have a handful of researchers begun to consider the situation from the perspective of incarcerated fathers, providing information on their characteristics (Hairston, 1995; Carlson and Cervera, 1992; Hairston, 1989) examining their affective states (Lanier, 1993) investigating father-child interaction (Lanier, 1991) or exploring parental attitudes (Hanrahan, Martin, Springer, Cox and Gido, 1996).

This study will build upon these earlier studies that have examined incarcerated parents and other studies that have explored the stress of confinement. The emphasis of the present study is parenthood – specifically fatherhood, and the ways in which being jailed impact the roles of men in their families, especially their roles as fathers. However, it must be acknowledged that for most individuals being confined is terribly stressful and that being separated from family is a stressful experience. Hence, this study will consider the experience of being a jailed father within the framework of the stress of confinement.

Jails

It is necessary to firmly establish that jails are very different from prisons. They serve a distinct function in the criminal justice process and house a more diverse population. The inmate population in our jails is a wide mix of convicted felons and misdemeanants, pretrial detainees, and inmates waiting transfer to a prison (Welch, 1994; Clear and Cole, 1990). "Jails have a very heterogeneous population made up of both males and females, adults and juveniles, who are often housed within the same facility" (Giever, 1997, p. 417).

Unlike prisons, which have a relatively stable level of admissions and releases, the jail has a revolving door nature, with a constant flow of individuals in and out. "From June 1989 to June 1990, there were nearly 20 million jail admissions and releases; clearly jails have more contact with the general population than do prisons" (Welch, 1994, p. 255). Consequently, our jail statistics are misleading because of the very transient nature of the population.

According to Welch (1994), our nation's jails serve a "social sanitation" purpose for our society by housing the "rabble" (Irwin, 1985) of our communities. In his book, *The Jail: Managing the Underclass in American Society,* Irwin (1985) contends that our jails are used to manage the underclass in American society, the poor, undereducated, unemployed and minority individuals in our communities.

Jails are locally administered and, unlike prisons, are usually found in or near the central business district (Giever, 1997). As a result, "unlike the prison inmate, the jail inmate is in close physical and psychological proximity to the outside community" (Gibbs, 1992, p. 181). This can result in significant stress for the jail inmate. "The jail inmate must be concerned with two worlds, although physically confined to one" (Gibbs, 1992, p. 182). The result is that the jail inmate is more keenly aware of, and psychologically tied to events in the outside world which can hamper adjustment to the inside environment (Gibbs, 1992).

Jail inmates face shorter sentences than do prison inmates. Among those inmates sentenced to jail in 1996, half received a sentence of just less than 9 months (Harlow, 1998). Because of their short-term nature, jails offer fewer programs and have access to fewer resources than do prisons. As a result, "jail overcrowding poses a more serious problem than prison overcrowding" (Welch, 1990, p.254). Overcrowding in our nation's jails results in a wide array of problems ranging from strains on classification and housing, to the delivery of food and medical services. Overcrowding impacts the daily routine of inmates and correctional personnel alike, increasing the level of stress and the likelihood of anger and hostility among both groups. "Jails are by their very nature stressful environments; overcrowding merely compounds pre-existing problems that result from warehousing too many persons in too little space" (Welch, 1994, p. 265).

Stress of Confinement

Incarceration is one of the most stressful experiences that a person can encounter (Sykes, 1958; Johnson and Toch, 1982; Lindquist and Lindquist, 1997). Inmates face the conditions inherent in a jail or prison setting, such as a rigid structure and rules, routinization of daily activities, and a loss of freedom. As Gresham Sykes (1958) points out, an institution is "a social system in which an attempt is made to create and maintain total or almost total social control" (p. xiv). Furthermore, incarcerated individuals face these conditions alone, as they are also separated from loved ones. Confinement is designed as a punishment, and punishment is painful.

It should be noted that confinement in one of our "modern correctional institutions" is seen by many as an improvement over the kinds of physical punishments that were used in times past (Sykes, 1958; Gilligan, 1997). However, incarceration is "aimed at punishing the person as a psychological and social being rather than solely a physical being" (Gilligan, 1997, p. 144). Consequently, the atmosphere within our correctional institutions may be more damaging to an inmate's psyche than his body. The environmental conditions that are common in jails and prison can be a significant source of stress for inmates (Johnson and Toch, 1988; Gibbs, 1986; Gibbs, 1987; Gibbs, 1991; Toch, 1992; Lindquist and Lindquist, 1997).

Stress is a difficult concept to define, but can be thought of as emotional arousal to "substantial changes in the environment" (Houston, 1985, p. 107). "Stress can be caused by physical elements such as bacteria, heat, cold, bone fractures, noise, crowding, and drugs. However, stress can also, and is often, caused by psychological factors, such as worry, anxiety, and guilt" (Houston, 1985, p. 109).

The United States has a wide array of correctional institutions – federal and state prisons of various security levels and treatment, along with local jails. Despite their distinctive characteristics, all institutions have common objectives – a focus on detention and confinement. Subsequently, most, if not all, incarcerated individuals experience the "pains of imprisonment" (Sykes, 1958) that result from existing in an environment that is lacking certain commodities commonly found outside the walls of an institution. According to Sykes (1958) inmates in correctional institutions face five common deprivations or frustrations. They are (1) the deprivation of liberty, (2) the deprivation of goods and services, (3) the deprivation of heterosexual relationships, (4) the deprivation of autonomy, and (5) the deprivation of security (pp. 65-78).

The reactions to these deprivations vary among individuals and are likely tempered by personal characteristics as well as external factors (e.g. the type of facility, overcrowding, contact with family). Many inmates experience anxiety, depression, loneliness, guilt, self-blame, and feelings of powerlessness and hopelessness (Cobean and Power, 1978; Carlson and Cervera, 1992). Often the length of time that an individual has been incarcerated will moderate the amount of stress felt (Cobean and Power, 1978). According to Cobean and Power (1978) inmates progress through three stages as they react to incarceration and separation from family. Each of these stages is marked by varying degrees of stress and accompanying reactions to that stress.

The initial confinement stage occurs during the first four to six weeks of incarceration and is marked by denial of the situation and feelings of anxiety for the inmate (Cobean and Power, 1978). It is during this stage that the inmate turns toward the community within the prison or jail in an attempt to forge new relationships and establish new roles (Sykes, 1958; Cobean and Power, 1978).

During the middle of imprisonment stage, the acute psychological impact experienced during the initial stage is replaced by general feelings of anxiety or depression and the boredom that accompanies the routine of institutional life (Cobean and Power, 1978). The stress of incarceration, though less acute than in the initial stage, is still present. The terminal stage of incarceration begins as the inmate nears release from the institution. "This stage is characterized by tension and anxiety. Memories, thoughts, and feelings about the home and community become conscious" (Cobean and Power, 1978). Successful reintegration into the community may well depend upon how well the inmate, and his family, navigates through this stressful situation (Cobean and Power, 1978; Carlson and Cervera, 1992).

It has been suggested that certain deprivations occur in all correctional settings (Sykes, 1958) and that inmates progress through several stages as they are adjusting to life behind bars (Cobean and Power, 1978). It has also been established that prisons and jails are very different settings and house different groups of people. Hence, it stands to reason that the experience of being jailed will be qualitatively different than the experience of being imprisoned, even though both forms of confinement have some common threads. For example, in prison, the middle of imprisonment stage, will likely last for a number of years, while in jail it will likely be counted in months. Jail inmates, in contrast to prison inmates, spend their shorter period of confinement in relatively close proximity to their families and communities, and thus may have an easier time during the terminal stage.

The same cannot be said of the initial confinement stage. For many individuals, jails are the "passageway" into a term of confinement. While most prisons receive inmates who have already been detained for a period, jails often receive individuals who have been living in their own homes and in relative freedom. "Entry into prison is gradual as compared with entry into jail" (Gibbs, 1992, pp. 177-178). The initial admission into jail is a chaotic, disorienting event in which an individual is stripped of his/her freedom and placed in confinement. This experience is very stressful and very different from entry into prison (Gibbs, 1986; Gibbs, 1988; Gibbs, 1992; Lindquist and Lindquist, 1997).

Entry into a jail also results in "rapid role transition" (Gibbs, 1992, p.186) as the inmate is also stripped of the roles he carried in the outside world – husband, father, son, brother, employee, and reduced to "inmate." According to Gibbs (1992) "arrest and detention are not designed to preserve a person's self-image, and few jail prisoners perceive themselves as powerful or potent figures in their new world" (p. 186). The result is often a reduction in the self-esteem and self-worth felt by the inmate.

The inmate must rely on family members and friends in the outside world for information and assistance with their case, as well as for support (visits, phone contact, commissary money, clothing) while confined. Heightened dependency on others reinforces the feelings of low self-worth and emphasizes the lack of control that the jailed inmate has (Gibbs, 1992).

The result for many individuals who are jailed is the experience of acute stress that may result in various forms of psychopathological symptoms. These symptoms are often directly related to the jail environment. More specifically, during the initial experience of being confined within the stressful jail environment, an individual may discover that the environment does not have the necessary attributes needed to reduce stress (Gibbs, 1992; Gibbs, 1991; Gibbs, 1987). Gibbs (1991; 1987) has suggested a "supply-demand congruence model" (1991, p. 371) in which each individual has various needs and the jail environment has limited resources in supply. To the extent that the individual's needs are met in this environment, stress will be reduced. However, to the extent that an individual's needs are unsatisfied, stress, and its accompanying symptoms, will remain.

In an extension of the work of Gibbs (1991; 1987), Lindquist and Lindquist (1997) examined gender differences in the level of stress experienced in the jail setting. The sample included 103 females and 95 males, of varying demographics, i.e. marital status, parental status, educational levels, that were housed in a large county jail. This study found that there were gender differences in the amount of psychological distress present – females reported higher levels of distress than did males. However, the reasons for the increased levels of distress were not clear. The researchers expected that mothers would suffer more because of their maternal roles and being separated from their children; this was not the case. More specifically, "being a parent (and separated from one's children) did not increase distress" (Lindquist and Lindquist, 1997, p. 522).

The findings from this study may cause some to question the utility of exploring further the extent to which being a parent influences one's mental distress while jailed. However, it should be noted that while Lindquist and Lindquist (1997) controlled for parental status, they did not control for the type of relationship that was in place prior to incarceration. Using "parent" as a variable relates solely to biological truths – fathering a child or giving birth to a child. However, it can be strongly argued that this biological event only makes an individual a "mother" or a "father," it does not make an individual a "parent". Parenting refers to developmental and social processes. It occurs over time and in interactions between adults and their children. It is a process, not a single event. Consequently, it is imperative to recognize that examining one's "parental status" and the level of stress that may result in a situation of confinement is not sufficient. It is necessary to fully understand the kind of "parent" an individual is in order to understand if "being a parent" influences the amount of stress one experiences when confined.

Families and Parenting

In American history, the family, and the roles and responsibilities of its members, has continually evolved. Over the last two centuries, families have shifted from patriarchal and extended (Bloom-Feshbach, 1981) to individualistic and unique. This transformation in social and family relations "brought a significant reduction in family and informal community functions, along with a decline in the authority of the father" (Bloom-Feshbach, 1981, p. 91).

As society advanced from an agrarian to an industrial state, there was a growing need for individuals to provide the necessary labor in industry. Men have made up the greatest proportion of our nation's workforce. This has resulted in a concurrent decline in the involvement of fathers in their families. Consequently, the modern father of the early to middle 20th Century, was cast as the family "provider", but experienced a decline in his authority and influence within his family (Benson, 1968). During this time frame, fathers spent more time at work and less time at home and in a parenting role. The father became an occasional supervisor and authority figure (Bloom-Feshbach, 1981).

Concurrently, many mothers worked at home and technological advances reduced the amount of time required to complete certain tasks. This permitted childrearing to become the primary focus of mothers (Bloom-Feshbach, 1981). "As the importance of motherhood steadily increased, there was a resulting downgrading of the paternal role. Many fathers began to serve essentially as disciplinarians of last resort... 'Wait till your father comes home'" (Stearns, 1978 as cited in Bloom-Feshbach, 1981, p. 95). Many devalued the father role, while others questioned if the father was necessary at all to his children's development (Bowlby, 1952).

Two important shifts have emerged during the second half of the twentieth century that have had a profound impact on the "traditional" American family. The first is the increase of mothers obtaining employment outside the home. The second is the soaring divorce rate. These two phenomena have served to force a shift of inquiry regarding the father's role in the family.

Since 1940, there has been a steady rise in the number of mothers in the labor force. As of 1999, 64.5% of women with children under the age of 6, and 78% of women with children between the ages of 6 and 17 were participants in the labor force (available online at http://www.dol.gov/dol/wb/public/wb_pubs/20fact00.htm). The shift of mothers to outside employment has placed a greater need to share childrearing responsibilities. Recent data from the U.S. Census Bureau suggests that some fathers are fulfilling this need. According to the Census Bureau report, fathers are responsible for taking care of one in every five preschool children while their mothers work (Chira, 1993). This, according to several childcare experts, confirms the increasing involvement of fathers in the raising of their children (Chira, 1993).

The second important shift has been the divorce rate in the United States. The United States has one of the highest divorce rates among industrialized countries (Guttmann, 1993). "In 1990, 1,175,000 marriages ended in divorce. If trends continue, three in five first marriages will be dissolved (Martin and Bumpass, 1989 as quoted in Arrendell, 1995, p. 23).

"Children are involved in approximately two-thirds of all divorces. In 1988, 1,044,000 dependent offspring experienced their parents' divorce; for each divorce decree in 1988, .89 minor children were involved" (Arrendell, 1995, p.23). Following a divorce, children are primarily under maternal custody (Arrendell, 1995; Guttmann, 1993), but this is changing. The proportion of single-parent families increased dramatically between 1970 and 1990 (from 11% to 24%), but has remained fairly stable since. In 1997, single parents headed 28% of all families in the United States. From 1990 to 1997, the number of female-householder families grew 17% and the number of male-householder families grew 33% (Bryson and Casper, 1998). While there are still many more children residing in single-mother families (12.8 million), the number of children residing in single-father families (3.8 million) is increasing at a greater rate. Father-headed families comprised 17% of all one-parent families in 1997, compared to 14% in 1990.

In addition to these shifts in the traditional family environment, "men are also seeking increased emotional closeness with their infants as part of a men's movement toward fuller personhood, and as a reaction against the alienation and burnout of the purely instrumental role of family provider" (Yogman, Cooley, and Kindlon, 1988, p. 53). Consequently, researchers have been forced to reevaluate the role the father plays in his children's development.

Theoretical Framework – Attachment Theory

Attachment theory developed as an offshoot of psychoanalytic theory and incorporates aspects of social learning theory, as well. John Bowlby, the individual most closely associated with attachment theory, "integrated ideas from psychoanalysis, ethology, experimental psychology, learning theory, and other sources to produce a theory that is having a major impact on studies of child development" (Hinde and Stevenson-Hinde, 1991, p. 52). This perspective differed from Freud's theory and proposed that infants were born with a biological need for protection by, and contact with, adults (Watkins, 1987; Lamb, 1981).

Bowlby distinguished between "attachment" and "attachment behaviors": "we can hardly state that there is attachment behavior until there is evidence that the infant not only recognizes his mother but tends to behave in a way that maintains his proximity to her" (1969, p. 199). Attachment behaviors begin to develop as early as four months and as late as twelve months (Watkins, 1987). The infant plays an important role in the development of attachment behavior, as he/she both reinforces and ignores parental behaviors.

Bowlby suggested that attachment behavior develops during infancy and young childhood but continues to be present throughout the life of the individual (Bowlby, 1988). An important feature of attachment behavior that is present at all ages is that the intensity and type of the emotion that accompanies it is dependent upon the strength of the relationship between the individual attached and the attachment figure. If the relationship is positive and strong, "there is joy and a sense of security" but if the relationship is strained or problematic, "there is jealousy, anxiety, and anger" (Bowlby, 1988, p.4).

Children who develop secure and loving relationships during their formative years will later generalize their cooperativeness and sociability to their interactions with others. Conversely, those children who do not form stable relationships will generalize their feelings of anxiety and insecurity in later years (Lamb, 1981).

The biological component is an important part of this theory. Both infant and parenting behavior have biological components, but both are tempered by experience. "Implicit in this approach is the assumption that parenting behaviour, like attachment behaviour, is in some degree preprogrammed and therefore ready to develop along certain lines when conditions elicit it" (Bowlby, 1988, p.4). Thus, parents have "urges" to respond to their children, but "all the detail is learned, some of it during interaction with babies and children, much of it through observation of how other parents behave, starting during the parent-to-be's own childhood and the way his parents treated him and his siblings" (Bowlby, 1988, p.5).

Adult parents' childhood experiences, particularly the parenting they experienced and the attachments they formed or failed to form, play a significant role in their subsequent parenting. Hence, childhood experiences play a large role in the adult behavior of parents. "There is strong evidence that how attachment behaviour comes to be organized within an individual turns in high degree on the kinds of experience he has in his family of origin, or, if he is unlucky, out of it" (Bowlby, 1988, p. 4).

Mary Salter Ainsworth "not only translated the basic tenets of attachment theory into empirical findings, but also helped us to expand the theory itself" (Bretherton, 1991, p. 9). Ainsworth did a number of studies of mother-infant attachment and provided valuable information regarding different patterns of attachment (Bretherton, 1991). Ainsworth developed the use of the *Strange Situation procedure*, a laboratory playroom "in which infants are observed responding to two brief separations from, and reunions with the parent" (Main, 1991, p.140). From this study, Ainsworth identified three patterns of attachment and corresponding behavior among the infants. The three patterns are (1) secure attachment, (2) insecure-ambivalent attachment, and (3) insecure-avoidant attachment (Main, 1991; Bowlby, 1988). Ainsworth compared the infant's behavior in the lab to observations of mother and infant interactions in the home. She discovered that there was a strong relationship "between maternal behavior in the home and infant response to the laboratory procedure" (Main, 1991, p.140).

In secure attachment, "the individual is confident that his parent (or parent figure) will be available, responsive, and helpful" in adverse situations (Bowlby, 1988, p. 124). In insecure-ambivalent attachment, "the individual is uncertain whether his parent will be available or responsive or helpful when called upon" (Bowlby, 1988, p.124). Because of this, the individual is prone to anxiety, especially separation anxiety, most likely because of the inconsistent responses from the parent. Finally, insecure-avoidant attachment is characterized by the individual having no confidence that the parent will respond in a helpful manner. In fact, the individual's mother constantly rebuffs him "when he approaches her for comfort or care" (Bowlby, 1988, p.125). Consequently, "he tries to become emotionally self-sufficient" (Bowlby, 1988, p. 124) to deal with repeated rejections.

While Bowlby and Ainsworth focused almost exclusively on the mother-child relationship, they did not deny that the child had the ability to form other relationships. Still, "it was several years before attachment theorists recognized that many infants formed significant relationships to both parents, even if the caretaker-infant relationship was the most important" (Lamb, 1981, p. 9). Evidence now suggests that both mother-infant and father-infant attachment are important to the development of the child (Lamb, 1981, Yogman, Cooley and Kindlon, 1988; Bronstein, 1988).

In 1981, Main and Weston used the "Strange Situation procedure" described above to examine mother-infant and father-infant attachment (Bowlby, 1988). They observed approximately 60 infants, first with one parent and then, about six months later, with the other. When comparing the two groups, the *patterns* of attachment between father and child closely resembled those between mother and child with a similar distribution percentage between groups (i.e. % of secure, % of insecure-ambivalent, and % of insecure-avoidant). Perhaps of more interest, the patterns shown by each child revealed *no* correlation between attachment to mothers and attachment to fathers. "Thus one child may have a secure relationship with the mother but not the father, a second may have it with the father but not the mother, a third may have it with both parents, and a fourth may have it with neither" (Bowlby, 1988, p. 10).

This study suggests that the father fills a role closely resembling the role filled by the mother – an attachment figure for his children, though there may be qualitative differences in the way he carries it out. "In most families with young children the father's role is a different one. He is more likely to engage in physically active and novel play than the mother and, especially for boys, to become his child's preferred play companion" (Bowlby, 1988, p. 11).

The central theme that comes into focus is that parents who are willing (accept and cherish parenthood) and able (are physically and emotionally present) to provide a "secure base" (Bowlby, 1988) for their children are most likely to rear children who feel safe and secure in the world and are most adaptive when venturing into it. In order to accomplish this, parents must have adequate time to devote to their children and must have had appropriate previous personal experiences with their own parents (Bowlby, 1988).

According to Bowlby (1988) parents who have had a disturbed childhood (e.g. being separated from their own parents) tend to engage in less frequent interaction with their own children than do parents with happier childhoods. Bowlby (1988) concludes that many patterns of disturbed parenting behavior (abusive and role-reversing) can be traced, in part, to childhood experiences.

From the above review several significant findings should be delineated. First, attachment theorists and researchers, like other individuals examining the parent-child relationship, until recently, have focused on the mother-child dyad (Lamb, 1981; Bowlby, 1988). Second, when the father-child relationship was the focus, it was discovered that children can and do form significant attachments to their fathers (Main and Weston, 1981) and the roles they fulfill are qualitatively different than the roles of mothers (Main and Weston, 1981; Yogman et al, 1988). Finally, the importance of the father's childhood experiences, especially the way he was parented, and the kind of attachment formed with his parents, will have a significant influence on his ability to parent, and the style of parenting he adopts with his own children (Bowlby, 1988).

We may make the reasonable conclusion that children who are reared in homes in which one parent is absent will be less able to form attachment to that parent, which will have an impact later in life. As outlined above, children's ability to form attachment to either parent is reduced or eliminated when the parent is absent. Interference with attachment is predicted to have negative effects on the child's life, including their ability to become effective parents. Our criminal justice policies have made parental absence a reality for an astonishing number of children, and the most affected relationship is the one between father and child.

THE FATHER-CHILD RELATIONSHIP

Recognition that the father-child relationship is crucial to the development of the child has led to an increasing interest among developmental researchers in examining this relationship, especially in the past two decades. This research has attempted to better understand when the relationship between father and child forms and to identify the distinctive characteristics of the father-child relationship that separate it from mother-child relationships (Lamb, 1981).

The research seems to indicate that both the mother-child and the father-child bonds form during infancy. The development of this attachment is critical to the later relationship between children and their parents. Overall, the empirical findings indicate that infants are attached to both parents, and that parents interact in qualitatively different ways with them (Yogman, Cooley, and Kindlon, 1988). Mothers tend to assume more nurturing, caregiving roles, while fathers tend to assume the role of the playful parent (Bronstein, 1988; Adler, 1997). Furthermore, children are able to distinguish among adults during infancy, and typically they become "calm in the presence of the mother, and aroused and stimulated by the approach of the father" (Adler, 1997, p.73). According to Dr. Kyle Pruett, a professor of psychiatry at the Yale University Child Study Center, parents hold or "cradle" children differently and play with them in different manners. While mothers tend to hold their infants in the same way, fathers tend to hold their infants in different ways, including upside down, each time they pick them up (Adler, 1997). Also, "mothers make more use of toys in playing with their children; fathers are more likely to employ their own bodies as portable, interactive monkey bars and rocking horses" (Adler, 1997, p. 73). Both of these roles are critical to the development of the child. "Even when they are the primary caregivers, fathers do not mother" (Pruett, as cited in Adler, 1997, p. 73).

As children age, the relationships between father-child and mother-child remain fairly constant. In other words, fathers continue to "play" more with their children while mothers continue to nurture and provide care. Fathers also tend to be "more verbally dominant and information-providing than mothers. Thus, in terms of gender-role socialization, fathers seem to be providing a particular model or prototype of male behavior, for boys to emulate and girls to eschew" (Bronstein, 1988, p. 118).

From these findings, one would suspect that the attachment and interaction between both dyads, mother-child and father-child, is qualitatively different and crucial for the development of the child. Also, the relationships will continue to grow and develop as the child ages.

Paternal Impact on Child Development

There is a growing belief among contemporary theorists and researchers that fathers play a crucial role in the psychosocial development of their children, especially their sons. Despite this belief and fairly extensive research in this area "the literature is extraordinarily inconclusive and contradictory" (Lamb, 1981, p.17).

In an excellent book chapter entitled "Fathers and Child Development: An Integrative Overview," Lamb (1981) summarizes and critiques the research that has focused on four areas of paternal influence on child development: (1) sex role development, (2) moral development, (3) achievement and intellectual development, and (4) social competence and psychological adjustment. Despite methodological problems in many of the studies reviewed, a few conclusions can be drawn with some confidence about the father's role in child development.

Every theory of parenting suggests that the father plays a major role in the sex role development of his children. Unfortunately, the research in this area has not been conclusive in suggesting exactly what that role is. "As far as sex role development is concerned, the father's masculinity and his status in the family are correlated with the masculinity of his sons and the femininity of his daughters. However, this association depends on the fathers' having sufficient interaction with their children - thus the extent of the father's commitment to childrearing is crucial"(Lamb, 1981, p.25).

In the area of moral development, there is less consensus among theorists and researchers. Research conclusions in this area have ranged from the father having little to no impact on a child's moral development to fathers being responsible for their children's delinquency (Lamb, 1981).

With regard to scholastic achievement, "there appears to be a correlation between the warmth of the father-child relationship and the child's academic performance" (Lamb, 1981, p.26). Finally, in the area of social and psychological adjustment, paternal warmth and sensitivity seems to be correlated to the successful social adjustment of both sons and daughters (Lamb, 1981). While conceptual and methodological problems have led to inconclusive results, the findings seem to indicate that the most effective and significant fathers will be those individuals who take their role seriously and are able to interact extensively, and warmly, with their children. Unfortunately, not every father desires, or is able, to interact with his children. Many children in our society grow up without the presence of their father. Researchers have attempted to grapple with this phenomenon to establish the effect of father-absence.

Father Absence

Being reared without a father figure is a situation many children face. Researchers have examined the impact of father absence on children, and have often examined the four areas of child development mentioned above (For a complete integrative overview, see Lamb, 1981).

Some of the studies that have examined father absence have looked at sex role development. The conclusions of these studies have indicated, "boys raised without their fathers are less masculine or else exhibit 'compensatory' hypermasculinity and aggressiveness. When the age at father-child separation is considered, studies show that father absence has the greatest effect on the masculinity of boys separated from their fathers in early childhood" (Lamb, 1981, p.27). In girls, father absence has been associated with problematic interactions with males, and appears to be more detrimental if the absence occurred early in the child's life (Hetherington, 1972).

Crumley and Blumenthal (1973) examined the effect on children of father absence due to military duty. The children in this study showed difficulty in social interactions. They found that both boys and girls exhibited more behavioral problems, school problems, and aggressiveness when the father was away.

Scholastic achievement has been the focus of some studies, and this, too, appears to be affected by paternal absence. According to Lamb (1981), "one of the more consistently reported effects of father absence on boys is a deterioration of school performance and intellectual capacity" (p.28).

Fathers are also considered to play a critical role in the moral development and behavior of their children (Parish, 1980; Santrock, 1975). Many researchers have suggested father absence is a contributing factor in the development of delinquent behaviors. Glueck and Glueck (1950) found that more than 40% of the delinquent boys in their sample were father absent compared with less than 25% of a matched nondelinquent group.

Despite some general interest in the topic, there have been very limited studies to assess the impact on children of father absence due to incarceration. Morris (1965) interviewed the wives of prisoners. According to these women, approximately 20% of their children exhibited increased behavioral problems following their father's incarceration. Swan (1981) studied 192 Black male prisoners' families in Alabama and Tennessee. The mothers in this study reported that the imprisonment of their husband had a major impact on approximately 30% of the children. For nearly 50% of the children, the mother's reported that the incarceration had little or no effect. Finally, Fritsch and Burkhead (1981) surveyed 38 fathers and 53 mothers incarcerated in a federal minimum-security prison regarding the occurrence of behavioral problems among their 194 children. The researchers found that the type of behavioral problems exhibited by the children was dependent on the gender of the incarcerated parent. Children of incarcerated mothers displayed "acting in" behaviors (such as withdrawal) while children of incarcerated fathers displayed "acting out" behaviors (discipline problems and hostility).

Several studies have indicated that deception regarding the father's incarceration is especially damaging to children, and may be a factor in the occurrence of disruptive behaviors (Gabel, 1992; Swan, 1981; Schwartz and Weintraub, 1974).

The studies designed to look at the issues surrounding father absence are not without their flaws. As Lamb (1981) points out, "research on the effects of father absence is characterized by a lack of methodological rigor" (p.29). Some of the flaws include a failure to consider other factors which may influence the child's behavior, such as the negative impact of the separation process itself (as in divorce), the timing of the paternal absence, and the reason for the absence.

Despite their weaknesses, the studies that have examined father absence are important for two reasons. The first is that those studies that have been methodologically sound have indicated a significant difference between children raised with fathers and those raised without fathers (Lamb, 1981). Second, "there is impressive congruence between these findings and the findings of studies employing other strategies to investigate the father-child relationship. Studies of father absence confirm that fathers influence sex roles, morality, achievement, and psychosocial adjustment" (Lamb, 1981, p.30). Unfortunately, in our society, many children are reared in households without fathers and parental divorce is a contributing factor is this phenomenon.

Divorce

There has been much written about families that have endured a divorce. While one can not suggest that divorce and incarceration affect family members in exactly the same manner, there are similarities, and much can be gained from looking at the abundant literature surrounding this societal phenomenon.

The divorce rate in the U.S. peaked in 1979 and 1981 at 5.3 per 1,000 (Guttmann, 1993). Since that time the divorce rate has decreased, and was 4.6 per 1,000 in 1994, according to the U.S. Census Bureau (http://www.census.gov/prod/2/gen/96statab/vitlstat.pdf).

In most instances of divorce, any children of the marriage reside with their mothers following the separation (Roman and Haddad, 1978; Guttmann, 1993; Arrendell, 1995). However, father-headed households continue to grow. According to the U.S. Census Bureau (Bryson and Casper, 1998), between 1970 and 1997 the number of male-headed families grew by 213%, from 1.2 million to 3.8 million. In 1997, 2,647,000 minor children resided with their fathers (Bryson and Casper, 1998).

There have been several studies that have examined families in the aftermath of divorce (for a complete overview, see Guttmann, 1993). Among the topics examined, the issue of father absence and its impact on children has been paramount[1]. Few of the studies, however, have acknowledged that all members of the family, including the father, are affected by divorce. In fact, the impact felt by fathers in the aftermath of divorce has been a neglected topic (Roman and Haddad, 1978; Arrendell, 1993; Guttmann, 1995).

Hetherington, Cox, and Cox conducted one of the studies that examined the reactions to divorce of both children and adults in the early 1970s. This longitudinal study focused on 96 families who had children of approximately 4 years of age at the time of the separation.

---

[1] See for example, Guttmann, J. (1993) Children of divorced parents: Theoretical and research considerations (chapter 6) in, *Divorce in psychosocial perspective: Theory and research.* Hillsdale, NJ: Lawrence Erlbaum Associates Publications.

The researchers of the project concluded that children of divorced parents were more "difficult": they tended to be more aggressive, whining, and emotionally distressed than other similarly aged children from intact families (as cited in Roman and Haddad, 1978).

In terms of the adults who had endured a divorce, the researchers found they also were affected. The women frequently complained of loneliness, felt a loss of social identity, and frequently felt overburdened with responsibility (Roman and Haddad, 1978). Fathers, on the other hand, had to cope with the loss of their wife and their children. Many did not fare so well. At least one third of the men in the Hetherington et al. study, who had previously been "highly involved, attached, affectionate parents reported that they could not endure the pain of seeing their children only intermittently and by two years after the divorce had coped with this stress by seeing their children infrequently although they continued to experience a great sense of loss and depression" (quoted in Roman and Haddad, 1978, p. 81).

More recently, Terry Arrendell (1995) conducted an exploratory study consisting of in-depth interviews with "75 divorced fathers living in various parts of New York state" (p. 4). Arrendell also noted the evolution of the *"fading father"* (p.143). "By their own reports, 9 of the 75 participants were absent fathers: They had neither seen nor had contact with any of their children during the past 12 months" (142). For these fathers, "withdrawal was both an actual practice and a perceived option and was an emotion management strategy" (Arrendell, 1995, p. 143).

For many fathers, being apart from their children is the most painful aspect of divorce and it significantly impacts their post-divorce adjustment (Guttmann, 1993). "The father's wish to remain significant in his children's life, on the one hand, and the painful experience associated with being a part-time parent, on the other, is probably the most difficult approach-avoidance conflict facing the divorced noncustodial father" (Guttmann, 1993, p. 126).

Separation from family members occurs for a variety of reasons and the impact of paternal absence appears to be very detrimental to both the children and fathers. Furthermore, there appear to be social class and racial differences, as "father absent" homes seem to be concentrated in specific areas and under specific conditions.

Suggestions of Social Class and Racial Differences

While the nuclear family is far from obsolete, many children are reared in environments that lack a father, or father figure. From 1970 to 1997, the number of female-headed households increased from 5.5 million to 12.8 million. The number of children under 18, living solely with their mother, now stands at 13,758,000 (Bryson and Casper, 1998). This family arrangement is prevalent among "African Americans, some Hispanic subgroups (most notably Puerto Ricans), and, to a growing extent, low-income whites as well" (Furstenberg, 1995, p. 119). According to Bumpass and Sweet (1989), most African American children "never reside with their biological fathers or reside with them only briefly; only a small minority live with them continuously throughout childhood" (as cited in Furstenberg, 1995, p. 120). "Father absent families are especially common among lower-class black families, surpassing 50 percent in some areas" (Biller, 1981, p.489). There are numerous structural factors in place in the United States that influence the rate of father absent households. For example, out-of-wedlock births, the divorce rate, and the incarceration rate will all have an impact on the number of children reared without a father. It is necessary to recognize that some groups are more affected by these factors than others.

Due in part to the macro-structural factors mentioned above, many fathers are not able or are unwilling to fulfill an active paternal role. Yet, a paradoxical picture emerges when one examines the growing number of fathers who are solely responsible for their children. According to the U.S. Census Bureau, the number of male-headed (single father) households tripled between 1970 and 1997, when there were 3.8 million male-headed households that were home to 2,647,000 minor children (Bryson and Casper, 1998).

It is difficult to reconcile these divergent data. According to Furstenberg (1995), two contradictory paternal trends have emerged over the past decade. "A growing number of fathers are retreating from the family at the very same time that others are becoming more involved parents" (Furstenberg, 1995, p. 120).   Hence, we are witnessing the simultaneous production of an increasing number of both "good dads" and "bad dads."   While social class does exert some influence on these patterns, "at all social levels parents are reinterpreting their responsibilities, resulting from a breakdown in the gender-based division of labor" (Furstenberg, 1995, p. 120). A number of forces may be responsible for heightened paternal commitment, including a cultural emphasis on fathering, increased need for fathers to share child-care responsibilities, and greater pressure on "deadbeat dads" to assume their financial obligations to their children (Furstenberg, 1995).

On the other hand, an increasing number of fathers are abandoning their parental responsibilities. The impact on the children in these situations is immense. "The great majority of fathers who live apart from their children see them infrequently and support them irregularly" (Furstenberg, 1995, p. 121). Economic stress may lead to more men adopting this parental strategy (Furstenberg, 1995) and may make the outcome for their children more damaging (Mosley and Thompson, 1995). According to Furstenberg (1995) "the 'good dads/bad dads complex' is best thought of as a set of conflicting cultural standards rather than as discrete packages of behaviors acquired by some men but not others" (p. 121).

Furstenberg (1995) undertook a study of African-American, inner-city youth to examine "how young parents construe paternal obligations and how they understand the barriers to fulfilling those obligations" (p. 122). The young adults in his study were "the offspring of women who initially had been featured in a study of adolescent parents in Baltimore" in the mid-1960s (Furstenberg, 1995, p. 122). Furstenberg (1995) did lengthy interviews with approximately 20 of the second-generation teen mothers and fathers.

Interestingly, there was unilateral consensus by both mothers and fathers on what it means to be a "good father." Many of the respondents suggested that fathers must "do for their children" (Furstenberg, 1995, p.124). This standard of "doing for your children" included: (1) being actively involved in their children's lives; (2) providing necessities for their children – financially; and (3) providing emotional support and involvement – spending quality time with their children. Unfortunately, " the absence of variation in men's and women's definitions of what being a good father meant contrasts starkly to men's performance as fathers" (Furstenberg, 1995, p. 125).

While some of the young men were able to remain involved in the lives of their children, they were the exception and not the rule. Most of the men in the Furstenberg (1995) study were not living up to their own standards of being a good father. However, "the men who stay involved with their children were esteemed by everyone...and those who do not are the object of much opprobrium" (Furstenberg, 1995, p. 127).

Furstenberg (1995) attempted to gain insight into how "young adults explain the relatively limited production of good dads" (p. 127). While many of the respondents suggested that developing as a father evolves over time, it became clear that the process of becoming a good father "is powerfully shaped by the acquisition of certain attitudes and habits in childhood. But the successful performance of the paternal role also requires men to negotiate a difficult series of adult transitions" (Furstenberg, 1995, p. 127). This suggests, once again, that the existence or absence of a bond between parent and child (attachment) is a critical component in the child's later parenting. However, other events and situations (e.g. poverty) that occur during life may strengthen or weaken this foundation. Hence, it can be concluded that attachment is generally a necessary, but is not a sufficient condition for "good fathering".

The beliefs that individuals develop about parenting are inextricably linked to their personal experiences. According to Furstenberg (1995), "conceptions of what inner-city fatherhood involves are drawn from personal history, participation in a culture where biological fathers rarely reside with their children, and exposure to mainstream American culture where images of fatherhood are in flux" (p. 128). Consequently, a cultural stereotype of African-American men as "missing fathers" (Pitts, 1999) has developed in this country. This image is "both generated internally from collective experience and also reflected and perhaps amplified by the way that African-Americans are generally portrayed in the mass media" (Furstenberg, 1995, p. 128).

The result is that many African-American men grow to adulthood lacking paternal role models, but face increasing cultural and societal pressure to be "good fathers" to their children. "Most men enter parenthood feeling that they have much to overcome and conscious that, to succeed, they must somehow defy the odds" (Furstenberg, 1995, p. 129). Thus, the path to effective parenting is most often an uphill struggle. When teenagers become parents, this struggle is amplified.

Many of the men in the Furstenberg (1995) study did not put much thought or planning into the decision of when to become a "father." Rather, many expressed surprise that their partners were pregnant. Furthermore, the relationships between the mothers and fathers in this study were often fairly casual. Consequently, "the commitment to paternity is fragile" (Furstenberg, 1995, p. 133). Because of the absence of a strong relationship between mother and father, the establishment and maintenance of the paternal relationship is more difficult. "Men's attachments to their children must be reinforced by women who barely know their children's father" (Furstenberg, 1995, p. 138).

While the young men and women in this study did not have stable relationships with one another, nearly all of them "placed a high value on lasting relationships, and many hoped to marry someday" (Furstenberg, 1995, p. 137). Hence, while these individuals lacked commitment to each other, they desired a committed relationship. Both men and women form partnerships with multiple individuals, perhaps in pursuit of the "ideal" relationship. Therefore, "it is not uncommon for young men to have fathered several children by different women" (Furstenberg, 1995, p. 139).

These young men, who have been reared in environments lacking a father, and who are involved in casual relationships when they become fathers, may feel completely overwhelmed and unprepared for what awaits after their child is born. Almost all of the men in this study "spoke of being emotionally undernourished by their biological fathers, leaving some feeling inadequately trained in how to be a caring father" (Furstenberg, 1995, p. 134). Though most of the men are sincere in their plans to "do for their children," many of them flee their parental responsibilities (Furstenberg, 1995).

Furstenberg (1995) queried the young women regarding the decisions that many men made to abandon their paternal role. They suggested a number of reasons to explain why men do not follow through on their pledges to "do for their children." According to the women, the men are (1) afraid to fail as fathers, (2) self-indulgent – which makes placing the needs of their children above their own needs difficult, and (3) immature. All of these explanations "have a common root in the socialization experiences of many young fathers in the inner city" (Furstenberg, 1995, p. 134).

Compounding all of this is the inability of many of the young fathers to be adequate providers for their children. In American culture, the father has been cast as the "provider" of his family (Benson, 1968). However, many young African-American men are unable to fulfill this role. In December 1994, "the unemployment rate for black youths 16 years old and older was 34.6 percent ...compared with a white youth unemployment rate of 14.7 percent, only 23.9 percent of all black youths were actually working, compared with 48.5 percent of white youths" (Wilson, 1996, p. 146). The result for many of these young men is that there are too few resources to meet competing and compelling demands.

Wilson (1996) argues that the disappearance of work (meaningful jobs) is a primary contributing factor to the disappearance of the married-couple family. Both men and women contribute to the decision not to marry. African-American women feel that African-American men lack dedication to their families and lack the ability to be adequate providers. Conversely, African-American men feel "that women are especially attracted by material resources and that it is therefore difficult to find women who are supportive of partners with a low living standard" (Wilson, 1996, p. 99).

"As employment prospects recede, the foundation for stable relationships becomes weaker over time" (Wilson, 1996, p. 105). More temporary arrangements become status quo, and these result in out-of-wedlock pregnancies and births. "The changing norms concerning marriage in the larger society reinforce the movement toward temporary liaisons in the inner city, and therefore economic considerations in marital decisions take on even greater weight" (Wilson, 1996, pp. 105-106). When there is a lack of commitment between partners, it is easier to find reasons to "not get married", and having limited employment and income are "reasons" to forego marriage.

It is apparent that cultural trends, such as greater acceptance of divorce and single parenting, are reflected, and perhaps magnified, when economic stress is present. "The evolving cultural patterns may be seen in the sharing of negative outlooks toward marriage and toward relationships between males and females in the inner city, outlooks that are developed in and influenced by an environment plagued by persistent joblessness" (Wilson, 1996, p. 106). The macro-level outcomes are weakened family structures, a higher number of out-of-wedlock births, increased reliance on governmental assistance (such as welfare and AFDC), and further erosion of the "parents as provider" role.

In addition to the economic factors outlined, there are other factors that influence marriage rates and the number of single parent families. Of particular interest for this project are incarceration rates, and it is necessary to recognize the disproportionate representation of African-American men in our prisons and jails.

The number of African-American men incarcerated in our nation's jails and prisons far exceeds their proportion among the U.S. population (King, 1993). While African-Americans comprise approximately 12% of the U.S. population, in June 1999 they comprised 44% of the state prison population and 41.5% of jail inmates (Beck, 2000) Over 12% of all black, non-Hispanic males between the ages of 25 and 29 were incarcerated in one of our nation's jails or prisons in 1999 (Beck, 2000). The United States has the highest incarceration rate of people of African descent in the world, exceeding the rate of indigenous Africans incarcerated in South Africa by four to one (King, 1993).

The incarceration rate of African-American men obviously affects this group's ability to participate in other social institutions such as colleges and universities. "On any given day in 1990, approximately 525,000 African American men were confined to jails or state or federal prisons. Similarly, on any given day, fewer than 480,000 African American men were enrolled in colleges or universities nationwide" (King, 1993, 146). Hence, there are more African-American men in jail or prison than in college. Educational attainment has a direct influence on one's ability to find meaningful employment in jobs with adequate income.

When a man is incarcerated his family members must deal with the stress that results from his imprisonment. According to King (1993), incarceration poses three major problems for families: (1) loss of income; (2) emotional and psychological distress; and (3) strain on the family structure. While all families may experience these problems, they pose even greater problems for African American families, many of which must additionally deal with racism, poverty, and community violence (King, 1993).

Many African-American men who are or have been incarcerated feel tremendous guilt over the fact that their incarceration is causing hardships for their families, and it is obvious that single-parent families face much greater hardships and disadvantages than do married-parent families. African-Americans comprise approximately 12% of the U.S. population, but 31% of all persistently poor families (defined as living below the poverty level during at least eight years in a ten year period) were headed by nonelderly African-American women (Wilson, 1996). Furthermore, the children in these families are "more likely to be school dropouts, to receive lower earnings in young adulthood, and to be recipients of welfare" (Wilson, 1996, p. 92).

Because there are greater numbers of African-American single-parent families facing these hardships, some individuals incorrectly assume that racial differences in parenting lead to the outcomes mentioned above. However, recent research of intact (two-parent) families indicates that even in the face of great economic hardship, parenting can counteract the adverse effects of poverty on children (Mosley and Thompson, 1995; Sampson and Laub, 1994).

Mosley and Thompson (1995) investigated the "effects of poverty and race on mothering, fathering, and child well-being" (p. 153) using the National Survey of Families and Households (NSFH). They limited their "analytic sample to married couples with children under 19 living in the household, with all of the children born to or adopted by the couple" (Mosley and Thompson, 1995, p. 153).

Mosley and Thompson (1995) found that poverty did not affect parental behaviors. In fact, poor parents were more actively involved with their children than were parents who were not living in poverty. Furthermore, "among original two-parent families, black children were reported to have better temperament or emotional outcomes than white children" (Mosley and Thompson, 1995, p. 158). While black and white fathers engage in activities with their children at about the same rate, black mothers "reported *less* frequent activities than white mothers, and parental control scores were higher for black families" (Mosley and Thompson, 1995, p. 158). This suggests that intact black families are very effective in fulfilling their parental roles and exert considerable influence over their children.

Furthermore, this study suggests that African-American two-parent families are very similar to white two-parent families. Hence, assumptions that there are "cultural" differences in parenting ability are not supported. On the other hand, poverty is likely to adversely affect children, especially if they do not have mothers *and fathers* to act as "buffers" for this stress. Thus, it is imperative that we stay focused on "the links between poverty and race rather than focused on race differences in family behaviors" (Mosley and Thompson, 1995, p. 164).

While the evidence indicates that intact African-American families can provide a "buffer" for their children from the poverty they may experience, many young African-American men and women forego marriage. Even though many of the young African-American men in our country have good intentions of becoming involved fathers, they discover a painful reality: "They are in no better position to assume fatherhood than their fathers were when they became parents" (Furstenberg, 1995, p. 146). In fact, they may be in a worse position due to the changing job market, where low skilled, mass production jobs have been replaced by "jobs in the highly technological global economy requiring training and education" (Wilson, 1996, p. 105).

Unless the cultural and economic processes that fuel many fathers' decisions to abandon their paternal roles are transformed, there is little hope of reversing the current "bad dad" trend. "If we continue to maintain the stratification that creates and sustains this culture, there is no hope of eradicating it by public exhortation or condemnation" (Furstenberg, 1996, p. 146). More children will grow to adulthood lacking paternal affection and interaction as their fathers fade from their lives. As Furstenberg (1995) has eloquently stated;

> When ill-timed pregnancies occur in unstable partnerships to men who have few material resources for managing unplanned parenthood, they challenge, to say the least, the commitment of young fathers. Fatherhood occurs to men who often have a personal biography that poorly equips them to act on their intentions, even when their intentions to do for their children are strongly felt, and fatherhood takes place in a culture where the gap between good intentions and good performance is large and widely recognized (p. 144).

Over the last twenty years, many areas in the United States have dealt with the loss of low-skilled mass production jobs as factories have closed. In many communities there is a "snowball" effect; there is a diminishing tax base, an out-migration of residents, and erosion in the surrounding infrastructure (including a decline in educational institutions). Unfortunately in this country, minority groups are affected by these structural factors at a disproportionate rate. The result for many individuals in these communities is a life plagued by poverty and its adverse effects.

Simultaneously, there has been an ongoing cultural trend toward acceptance of diverse family arrangements, including single parenting. When economic stress is present, these cultural trends are amplified and the foundation for stable and long-term relationships is weakened (Wilson, 1996). Hence, in situations where poverty is a way of life, so too, is single parenting. Because there is a greater proportion of minorities (African-American, Latino, Native American, etc) impacted by the aforementioned macro-structural factors, they are also over represented among single parents and, consequently, among father-absent families. "Race" (biology) has become the proxy variable used to allude to these underlying macro-structural factors. The problem inherent with this approach is that many individuals (researchers and lay individuals, alike) conclude that there must be "racial" differences in parenting ability and behavior. This is not accurate.

Recent research that examined the effect of race and poverty on fathering behavior and child outcomes found that race was not a significant variable. (Mosley and Thompson, 1995). The authors further concluded that the adverse effects of poverty are real, and that these conditions require "extra effort on the part of the parent to buffer children from economic stress" (Mosley and Thompson, 1995, p. 164). The researchers found that intact black families were more successful as "buffers" to economic stress than were intact white families (Mosley and Thompson, 1995). Furthermore, fathers in low-income, intact families are nearly twice as likely as fathers in higher-income, intact families to provide care for their children while their wives work (Casper, 1997). This is true for families of all races. This suggests that regardless of race or income-level, intact families can exert considerable influence over their children and can "buffer" their children from the adverse effects of poverty. More importantly, fathers play a critical role in this process. This research speaks directly to the issue of race and suggests that it is not one's racial makeup, but rather structural factors, such as poverty, that influence parenting and child outcomes.

In summary, the available evidence, discussed above, suggests that the father plays a crucial role in the well being of his children, and that his presence may be especially critical when economic stress is present. It seems likely that the impact of a father's absence will affect his children not only during their childhood, but when they are grown and raising children. Despite this evidence, we have failed to acknowledge the existence of a very substantial, yet invisible group of absent fathers: incarcerated men.

INCARCERATED FATHERS

As mentioned previously, the majority of research in corrections focuses on prison inmates rather than jail inmates. Additionally, if researchers are interested in family and separation issues, they focus on incarcerated mothers rather than incarcerated fathers, which suggests that our cultural beliefs that mothers are the "critical" parents are reflected in criminological inquiry. Consequently, there is much more information available on imprisoned mothers than is available on incarcerated fathers. Furthermore, almost all of the information regarding incarcerated fathers has been collected from men who are incarcerated in prisons.

The majority of men incarcerated in the United States are parents. In 1997, 55% of the men imprisoned in state facilities and 63% of the men imprisoned in federal facilities had minor children. In 1999, there were an estimated 667,900 fathers in our prisons and these men had an estimated 1,372,700 minor children (Mumola, 2000). Unfortunately, there are no national estimates on the number of jailed fathers. However, by using the percentage of imprisoned fathers nationwide (55%) and applying this to the male jail population, we can cautiously estimate that there are an additional 295,942-jailed fathers nationwide. Because of the "revolving door" nature of jails, the absolute number of fathers in jail over the course of a year is much higher.

Forty-four percent of the fathers incarcerated in state prisons lived with their children prior to incarceration. About 90% of the incarcerated fathers reported that their minor children resided with their mothers while the father served time. Over 60% of parents in state prisons were housed more than 100 miles from their last place of residence. In spite of this, 52% of inmate fathers had contact with their children at least once a month (Mumola, 2000).

These fathers share many characteristics with other inmates. They are low-income, poorly educated individuals with limited job skills and employment opportunities. Many had been separated from their own parents as children, and have dealt with substance abuse/addiction issues, and other traumatic experiences including abuse, parental alcoholism/addiction, and the incarceration of a family member (Beck et al, 1993). In recent years, a handful of researchers have begun to examine these invisible parents – incarcerated fathers.

Specific Studies That Examine Incarcerated Fathers

As mentioned previously, there is very limited information on incarcerated fathers. To date, all studies have focused on prison inmates. The available studies are listed in Table 1. What follows is a thumbnail sketch of the studies, and then a discussion of the findings.

Bakker, Morris and Janus (1978) interviewed the wives of seven men who were incarcerated either in jail or prison in California. The wives provided details of how their husbands' incarceration had affected their lives. This was one of the first studies to examine these concerns. Laura Fishman (1990) provided a more detailed account of the struggles facing wives of prisoners in her book, *Women at the Wall.*

Fritsch and Burkhead (1982) surveyed a group of prisoners in a federal minimum-security prison in Lexington, Kentucky. Ninety-one of the prisoners in this group were parents; 38 fathers and 53 mothers. They had a total of 194 minor children. The study examined the parents' perceptions about their children's behavioral reactions to parental incarceration.

Koban (1983) studied 206 men and women in a Kentucky prison. One hundred eleven were fathers and 95 were mothers. She compared the effects of imprisonment on the parent-child relationships between incarcerated fathers and incarcerated mothers and their respective children.

Table 1: Studies of Incarcerated Fathers

Year	Author(s)	Setting	Method	Sample size	Topic
1978	Bakker, Moris & Janus	Not applicable	Interviews with wives of prisoners	N = 7	Problems facing families of incarcerated men
1981	Fritsch & Burkhead	Federal Minimum sec. prison	Survey of incarcerated fathers and mothers	N = 91 n = 38 fathers	Parents perceptions of children's behavioral reactions
1983	Koban	Two medium sec. female prisons and two medium sec. male prisons	Survey of incarcerated mothers and fathers	N = 206 n = 111 fathers	Compared the effects of incarceration on the families of mothers and fathers
1989	Hairston	Maximum sec. prison	Survey of male inmates	N = 115	Family charac-teristics and parenting views
1991	Lanier	Maximum sec. prison	Survey of male inmates	N = 302	Father-child interaction
1992	Carlson & Cervera	3 Max. and 2 Med. sec prisons	Interviews with inmates and wives	N = 63 inmates and 39 wives	Incarceration and family life
1993	Lanier	Maximum sec. prison	Survey of male inmates	N = 302 n = 188 fathers	Affective States of incarcerated fathers
1995	Hanrahan, Martin, Springer, Cox &Gido	Medium Security prison	Survey of imprisoned fathers	N = 104	Child rearing practices and parenting styles
1995	Hairston	1 Minimum and 1 Max. sec. prisons	Surveys of imprisoned fathers	N = 126	Family relationships and parenting concerns

39

Hairston (1989) surveyed 115 men imprisoned in a maximum-security prison in a Southeastern state. There were 96 fathers in the group who were parents to 246 children. The survey focused on family characteristics, contact with children, and parenting skills.

Lanier (1991) surveyed 302 men imprisoned in a maximum-security prison in New York State. The focus of the study was to examine father-child interaction during parental incarceration.

Carlson and Cervera (1992) interviewed 63 men incarcerated in New York State Prisons (three maximum-security facilities, and two medium security facilities). Additionally, the authors interviewed the wives of 39 prisoners. The focus of the study was to examine the impact of incarceration on inmate families, and to identify methods of coping used by married inmates and their wives to survive the stresses associated with the imprisonment of a husband and father.

Lanier (1993) surveyed 302 men imprisoned in a maximum-security prison in New York State. 188 of the men were fathers. The focus of this study was to examine the affective states of fathers separated from their children by imprisonment.

Hairston (1995) surveyed 92 men imprisoned in a maximum-security prison and 34 men imprisoned in a medium security prison. The focus of this study was to define the nature of prisoners' family ties, to identify their parenting concerns and to assess their interest in organized family programs

.Finally, in a pilot study for the current project, Hanrahan, Martin, Springer, Cox and Gido (1996) surveyed 104 fathers imprisoned in a medium security prison (See also Martin, Hanrahan, Gido and Moloney, 1995). The focus of this study was to examine the child rearing practices of the fathers and to administer a parenting inventory (AAPI) designed to look at the parenting styles of the fathers.

FINDINGS FROM PRISON-BASED PARENTING STUDIES

Family characteristics

The majority of imprisoned fathers were not married to the mothers of their children (Hairston, 1989; Lanier, 1993; Hanrahan, et al, 1996; Hairston, 1995). Over one-half of the inmates in Hairston's study

(1995) reported that their marriages had ended during their current incarceration.

Inmate fathers had, on average, 2.3 to 2.6 children (Hairston, 1989; Lanier, 1993; Hairston, 1995) and many of these are minor children (Lanier, 1993; Hanrahan et al, 1996; Hairston, 1995). In some instances, the fathers had children with more than one woman (Hanrahan et al, 1996; Hairston, 1995). In the Hanrahan et al study (1996) a full 69% of the fathers were living with a child at the time of their arrest.

Prison Visits and other contact

Most of the imprisoned fathers seldom see their children (Hairston, 1989; Lanier, 1991; Hairston, 1995). However, each of the three studies that noted this had studied fathers incarcerated in maximum-security prisons. While 25% of the fathers in the Lanier (1991) study saw their children at least once a month, another 32% of the inmate fathers in this group had never been visited by their children during their incarceration. Similarly, 30% of the fathers in the Hairston (1995) study had not seen their children at all during their incarceration, and "fewer than one-half had seen their children in the 6 months preceding the survey" (p. 35). Conversely, in the Hanrahan et al study (1996) 64% of the men reported that they had visited them at least once during their incarceration. It should be noted that this study was conducted in a medium security prison.

There may be several factors for the lack of face-to-face contact. In many states, institutions are located in remote areas that would require transportation for family members who are often located in urban centers. If a family does not have an automobile, it may be impossible to visit. Even with an automobile, the distance between home and prison most likely would make traveling time-consuming and costly, especially with children. For many inmate families, visiting is not a viable alternative.

Perhaps of greater importance, some incarcerated fathers terminate contact with their children (King, 1993, Koban, 1983). In Koban's (1983) study of federal prisoners 87% of the unvisited fathers claimed that it was their decision to forego contact. This may indicate a lack of concern for their children, or it may suggest that sporadic contact is too difficult and painful for the fathers to endure.

Telephone contact is an important mode of family contact for inmate fathers. Many institutions do not permit incoming telephone calls so inmates must place collect calls to their family members. This can be an expensive burden for the family. Still, a large majority of inmate fathers maintain regular telephone contact with their wives and children (Lanier, 1991; Carlson and Cervera, 1992; Hanrahan et al, 1996). In the Carlson and Cervera (1992) study the most common topic of telephone conversation between imprisoned husbands and their wives was their children.

Written correspondence was another way that inmate fathers maintained contact with their children, and children maintained contact with their dads (Lanier, 1991; Carlson and Cervera, 1992). This seemed to be a significant form of communication for many of the prisoners (Lanier, 1991). Again, in written communication between husband and wife, the children were the most frequent topic (Carlson and Cervera, 1992).

In the Carlson and Cervera (1992) study, the imprisoned fathers believed that maintaining communication had a positive influence on the family, while the wives were less certain of the positive impact. According to the authors, perhaps the contact "reminded them [wives] of how hard their life on the outside is, or the inmate made requests of her that created real hardships" (p. 68). It is also possible that the phone contact was intrusive and an attempt by some inmates to maintain control over their wives from inside the prison (Fishman, 1990).

Finally, visits and contact between imprisoned fathers and their children is dependent upon the father's pre-incarceration residence and relationship with his children and their mother(s) (Hairston, 1989; Lanier, 1991; Hairston, 1995). Fathers who lived with their children prior to incarceration are more likely to maintain contact during imprisonment (Lanier, 1991). Also, a man's marital status is linked to whether or not his children visit. According to Hairston (1989), "62% of the married fathers had regular visits from their children, only 20% of the single fathers did" (p. 27).

Impact on family members

A man's incarceration has a significant, and most often negative, impact on his family members (Bakker, Janus and Morris, 1978; Fritsch and Burkhead, 1981; Carlson and Cervera; 1992, Hanrahan et al, 1996). Wives of inmates identify financial hardships, housing concerns, and lack of childcare assistance as major problems they face (Bakker, et al, 1978). Consequently, many of these women turn to their extended families for help (Carlson and Cervera, 1992).

According to the inmate parents in the Fritsch and Burkhead study (1981), children also suffer as a result of parental incarceration. When children were aware of their parents' incarceration, they often exhibited varied behavioral problems. Interestingly, the type of behavioral change seemed to be related to the gender of the incarcerated parent. If a child's mother was incarcerated, the child displayed "acting in" behaviors (withdrawal, daydreaming, fear of school, crying a lot). Conversely, if a child's father was incarcerated, the child exhibited "acting out" behaviors (hostility and aggressiveness, drug and alcohol use, school truancy, running away). The parents reported "problems with their children in precisely those areas where they would traditionally accept major responsibility for the rearing of children if living at home" (Fritsch and Burkhead, 1981, p. 86). Of further importance, in the Fritsch and Burkhead study (1981) inmates who had contact with their children both prior to and during incarceration were more likely to report the occurrence of behavioral problems among their children.

In the Hanrahan et al study (1996) eighty percent of the inmate fathers reported that their children's behavior had been impacted during their incarceration. The fathers also reported that their children were worse off emotionally and financially as a result of their incarceration.

Parenting

According to the findings, there is strong agreement that the fathering role was an important one for inmate fathers (Hairston, 1989; Carlson and Cervera, 1992; Lanier, 1993). The majority of inmate fathers resided with their children prior to their incarceration (Carlson and Cervera, 1992; Lanier, 1993; Hanrahan et al, 1996) and reported they spent "a lot" of time with them pre-incarceration (Lanier, 1993). The fathers in the Carlson and Cervera study (1992) reported feeling very close to their children and had "an awareness of essential elements of the father role despite the fact of being incarcerated" (p. 83).

Also, most of the fathers had played a prominent role in decision making regarding their children prior to incarceration, and maintained some of the child-related decision making during incarceration (Carlson and Cervera, 1992). Still, the separation that occurred as the result of the father's imprisonment resulted in "significant decay in the relationships with their children" (Lanier, 1993, p.56) and, for many fathers, this is a devastating result of their imprisonment (Hanrahan et al, 1996).

One of the explanations offered by the authors for the reports of a warm and involved relationship between father and child(ren) was social desirability (Carlson and Cervera, 1992). As the authors point out, "many of these inmates are undoubtedly sophisticated enough to know that it is not socially acceptable today to admit lack of investment in the father role. However, such awareness would be noteworthy in a marginal population such as this one" (1992, p. 83).

Lanier (1993) suggests that it is possible that the prison setting permits inmate fathers much time to reflect; and absent other close relationships, this might cause the father-child role to "increase in importance for the fathers during the period of imprisonment" (p. 60).

The fathers reported frequent contact, often via telephone, with their children during imprisonment (Hairston, 1989; Carlson & Cervera, 1992; Lanier, 1993). As a result, the closeness between father and child reported by the inmates may be a reflection of the frequent communication. "Thus, these regular forms of contact may enable these inmates to maintain feelings of closeness to their children despite being incarcerated" (Carlson & Cervera, 1992, p. 84).

Finally, it is possible that the inmate fathers in the aforementioned studies were being the best fathers that they knew how to be. Most inmates are low-income individuals while most researchers are not. It is problematic to apply middle-class standards to the parenting behavior and experiences of individuals who are not in that economic standing. Parents in general, and fathers specifically, are likely to be more highly involved with their children when economic hardship is not present. It is possible that many of the inmate fathers had close relationships with their children prior to their incarceration, and the relationship that they share with their children is genuinely important to them.

If this final explanation is accurate, this raises two questions to be addressed by this study: (1) how are inmate fathers affected by the separation from their children? (2) do the pre-incarceration relationships between inmate fathers and their children influence the stress experienced during confinement?

Summary of Findings From Prison Based Studies

There are several things that emerge from a review of the literature on incarcerated fathers. The first thing that becomes apparent is the dramatic lack of information. There is a clear gap in our knowledge regarding incarcerated fathers. Second, it is important to note that many of the studies have viewed the incarcerated father as the independent variable and the effect of his incarceration on his family as the dependent variable (Bakker, Janus, Morris, 1978; Swan, 1981; Fritsch and Burkhead, 1981; Koban, 1983; Carlson and Cervera, 1992). While this research is valuable in its own right, it tells us very little about the incarcerated fathers themselves.

Third, the information that is available focuses on imprisoned, rather than jailed fathers. In many instances these fathers were facing long terms of imprisonment and similarly long terms of separation from their children and other family members. For example, in both of the studies carried out by Hairston (1989; 1995) the overwhelming majority (70% and 67% respectively) of her samples were serving terms of 20 years or more. For many of these fathers, their children will grow to adulthood while they complete their sentences.

Fourth, visitation is sporadic due in part to the distance between home and prison and the difficulty that this presents for family members. Despite the lack of regular proximal visits, the fathers were able to maintain contact through telephone conversations and written correspondence. This seemed to be meaningful for the fathers and permitted them a way to maintain some type of relationship, however "distant" it may be. It is probable that visitation is more frequent between jailed fathers and family members however, because jails are located in closer proximity to the inmates home and family, which should enhance visitation opportunities. Also, sentences are shorter and this should enhance an inmate's ability to maintain a relationship with his spouse or significant other, and their children. It may also increase the likelihood of a wife or significant other's willingness to remain in a relationship, since one can "see the light at the end of the tunnel."

While the limited literature concerning inmate fathers provides a sketch of the issues concerning this understudied group, it seems to raise more questions than provide answers. The research questions were guided by the theoretical framework of attachment theory and by recent research on single parent families. The goals of this study are two-pronged. One goal is to begin to develop a fuller understanding of the experiences and perceptions of these invisible fathers. The second is to apply the information gathered to suggest policy and programmatic initiatives.

The overarching question is, "How does the experience of being jailed affect the role of men in their families, especially their roles as fathers?" It will be necessary to gather information on pre-incarceration relationships, as well as the maintenance of these relationships during incarceration. Thus, the more specific questions are as follows:

1) What are the social and family characteristics of the inmate fathers' family of origin?

2) How were the inmate fathers' parented during their childhood?

3) What are the characteristics of the pre-incarceration relationships of jailed fathers in their families?

4) What is the nature and significance of contact with family during incarceration?

5) Do the pre-incarceration relationships of jailed fathers impact the stress of incarceration?

6) What are the jailed fathers' plans and expectations regarding their paternal role following release?

CHAPTER 2
Methods

INTRODUCTION

This study was undertaken with several broad objectives in mind. The first was to develop a better understanding of the characteristics of jailed fathers, including information on their families of origin and their present family structures. A second objective was to explore the importance and salience of the parenting role for jailed fathers and to investigate the unique impact of incarceration on parenting. A final objective was to explore a set of issues identified in the literature as relevant: (1) the nature of the fathers' childhood experiences and the way that these experiences influence their parenting behavior; (2) and the extent to which pre-incarceration parental relationships, and contact with family during incarceration, influence the stress of the jail experience.

These objectives fit into the research agenda proposed by Lanier (1995) in his article, *Incarcerated fathers: A research agenda*. In this article, Lanier emphasized that research focusing on incarcerated fathers should "explore the importance placed by incarcerated fathers on their parental role. This research should assess the incarcerated parent's current and pre-incarceration relationships, as well as looking at the varying lengths of separation on the father-child relationship" (available online: http://www.csc-cc.gc.ca/crd/forum/e072/e072k.htm).

This project is an exploratory/descriptive study of inmate fathers that was conducted as a two-phase process. The first phase of the project consisted of the group-administration of questionnaires to 105 jailed fathers in the two research sites described below. The second phase consisted of 26 in-depth interviews with inmate fathers[2].

SAMPLING

There are two basic issues related to sampling in this project. The first is the selection of research sites and the second is the selection of individual participants at those sites. The procedures employed in both aspects of sampling are described below.

Site Selection

As discussed earlier, jails serve a very distinct function within the criminal justice system and they house a very diverse population. Unlike prisons, which have relatively stable populations, jails have much more transitory populations, with millions of individuals passing through on an annual basis (Welch, 1994). Additionally, "jails remain one of the most understudied and widely misunderstood agencies within the system" (Giever, 1997, p. 416). There have been no previous studies that have focused on jailed fathers. Consequently, despite the large number of men who are jailed in this country, very little is known about this group.

The selection of research sites for this study was guided by both methodological and pragmatic concerns. This study focused on fathers housed in two Western Pennsylvania jails. The Commonwealth of

---

[2] Consideration was given to employing focus groups as a means of gathering information from jailed fathers regarding the parental role. There was concern, however, that the jail setting may not be optimal for conducting such groups (their participation cannot be anonymous or confidential). Some inmates, perhaps especially men, may be reluctant to discuss issues regarding their family in a group setting. Furthermore, there are often power structures present in correctional facilities and these may influence focus groups.

Pennsylvania is comprised of 67 counties. Nearly every county has its own jail (two smaller counties have closed their facilities), and Philadelphia County has multiple facilities that make up the Philadelphia County Jail. Therefore, the Commonwealth of Pennsylvania has a minimum of 67 jails, which in 1994 housed 19,756 inmates (Bleyer, 1995).

The counties in Pennsylvania are divided into eight classes based on their civilian population and the county jails are categorized in the same manner (personal communication, Warden Carol Wilson, 2-26-99). Class 1 represents the largest county and Class 8 corresponds to the counties with the smallest civilian populations. The Commonwealth of Pennsylvania has one Class 1 county jail and one Class 2 county jail (See Table 2). The Class 1 county jail is located in Philadelphia County, and the Class 2 county jail is located in Allegheny County, which incorporates the city of Pittsburgh. These two county jails housed 30.8% (n = 6078) of the total jail population in 1994 (Bleyer, 1995).

Table 2: Pennsylvania Jails, by Class Size and Daily Population

	Number	Percent	1994 ADP
Class 1	1	1.50%	4809*
Class 2	1	1.50%	1278*
Class 2A	3	4.47%	934.67
Class 3	11	16.42%	571.45
Class 4	7	10.45%	175.57
Class 5	9	13.43%	175.77
Class 6	22	32.83%	64.68
Class 7	7	10.45%	49.50
Class 8	6	8.95%	24**
Total	67	100.00%	19,756***

* Because there is only one facility, these are not averages
** Information available for only 2 of the 6 Class 8 jails
*** 1994 Average Daily Population for all 67 jails
Derived from the 1994 County Statistical Report (Bleyer, 1995).

Class 6 is the classification with the largest number of jails; twenty-two of the remaining 65 county jails are classified in this category (See Table 2). These jails are in counties with populations of fewer than 90,000 civilians (personal communication, Warden Carol Wilson, 2-26-99). Thirty-three percent of all jails in Pennsylvania are Class 6 facilities. In 1994, the average daily population for a Class 6 jail was 64.68, with a population range of 27-173 (Bleyer, 1995). Hence, the modal category of Pennsylvania jails is comprised of relatively small facilities and the first research site is one of these facilities.

At year-end, 1994, the majority (56.3%, n=11,015/ N=19,552) of the jail inmates in Pennsylvania were "non-white," with most of these inmates (82.3%, n=9,066) being African American. The two largest jails in Pennsylvania (Philadelphia county and Allegheny county) housed 55% (n = 4,981) of all of the African American jail inmates in 1994. Hispanics made up 15.5% (n= 1,710) of the minority jail population and the remaining 2.2% (n = 239) consisted of other racial or ethnic minorities. The overwhelming majority of Hispanic inmates were housed in county jails in Eastern Pennsylvania. For example, in 1994, Philadelphia County housed 414 Hispanic inmates while Allegheny County housed none. The remaining Pennsylvania jail inmates (43.7%, n = 8,537) in 1994 were white (Bleyer, 1995).

The study sites were drawn from Western Pennsylvania jails for pragmatic reasons. The first site was selected because it is a Class 6 jail, the most common jail size in the Commonwealth of Pennsylvania. Because African Americans comprise nearly 50% of the jail inmates in Pennsylvania, it was necessary to be certain that African American fathers were represented in the study sample. Thus, the second site selected was a large, urban jail. It was included to ensure racial diversity in the study sample.

Participant Selection Variables

For the purposes of this project, a jail inmate was deemed a "father" if he had any children. A "child" included biological, adoptive, and stepchildren, along with any child for whom the inmate was a legal guardian. Finally, if the inmate was involved in a "living together" relationship prior to incarceration, the minor children of an inmate's significant other were included. A father was identified as a "parent" if he (a) resided with all of his children during the six months prior to incarceration, or (b) had substantive (daily) contact with a child during the six months prior to incarceration. Men who did not reside with any of their children were identified as "biological fathers," and men who resided with some of their children but not all of their children were deemed "mixed parents" for this project.

All variables were operationalized by securing responses to specific questions on the survey or through the interview.

PHASE I – SURVEY

Recruitment and Sampling

The process for recruiting respondents was determined, in part, by the administration of each site and the design of the respective facility. Thus it is necessary to briefly describe each facility. The urban jail went on line in the spring of 1995. This is a large facility, both in physical size and in the number of inmates that are housed within it. The facility is approximately 900,000 square feet under one roof and houses approximately 1,650 inmates per day (personal communication, Lt. Frank Fraietta, 4-1999). There are 35 housing units (pods) in the facility, and the inmates are assigned to one of these units based on an objective classification system. The jail is a fairly complex organization that consists of a management system divided into three major divisions: Operations, Program Services, and Administration (Allegheny County Jail – Annual Report, 1997).

The researcher worked in collaboration with the Deputy Warden and Assistant Deputy Warden of Program Services during this project. Access was granted to 4 of the 35 pods based on security concerns. All of the pods that were accessible housed inmates considered to be low security risks. Two of the pods were "worker" pods, and the inmates housed there had jobs within the jail. Hence, they were able to leave their housing units in order to work. This feature was unique to these two pods. The other two housing units were "program" pods, meaning that the inmates on these pods had access to a variety of programs including AA/NA and parenting information. There is one correctional officer staffing each of the housing units and he/she works an 8-hour shift. Thus, there are three different correctional officers each day in each housing unit.

The researcher spoke with each of the "daylight" correctional officers to determine the best way to announce the project in their respective housing unit. Flyers announcing the project were placed on the housing units. Inmates were asked to indicate interest by signing up on the accompanying sign-up sheet. Some problems were encountered with this process, such as the sign-up sheets being lost or misplaced or removed by the correctional officers with whom the researcher did not have the opportunity to speak. For example, the "overnight" correctional officer may have removed the flyer but failed to tell the next officer where he placed the information. When the researcher returned, there was no information to indicate which of the inmates had signed up to participate in the project. In these situations, the researcher would simply announce her presence and request volunteers. This alleviated the problem for the correctional officers of keeping track of a piece of paper.

An additional problem was encountered in the "working" pods; work schedules reduced the number of available respondents. The inmates worked in three shifts. Consequently, when the researcher arrived at the housing unit in mid-morning, approximately one-third of the unit's inmates were at work and another one-third was asleep because they had worked overnight. Thus, approximately one-third (20-25) of the housing unit's population was available on any given day and not all of them were eligible or willing to participate. Furthermore, the inmates worked the same schedules, so the same men were available each time the researcher was present. As a result, there are fewer respondents from the "working" pods.

The "program" pods resulted in the greatest number of participants for two reasons. First, the inmates were unable to leave the units, so there were 60-70 men available on a daily basis. Also, the correctional officers on these two housing units had good rapport with the inmates and were exceptionally accommodating with the researcher. For example, they assisted in setting up for the group administration of the questionnaire, they announced the project over the loudspeaker, and they even altered the schedule within the unit so that there were no conflicting demands (programs) for the inmates (e.g. on one occasion they moved the AA/NA meeting to a later time so that those inmates had the opportunity to participate in the research project if they so desired). As a result, the two "program" pods provided the researcher with the majority of the respondents in this study.

The Class 6 jail is located in a rural setting and is a much smaller facility, housing approximately 70 inmates on a daily basis. The jail administration arranged for the individual who provided programming for the inmates to announce the study and present information about participating in it. This individual would then notify the administration of interested inmates, and they would then notify the researcher. Numerous attempts were made to enlist participants from this site, but the size of the facility greatly impacted the number of participants.

The sample for Phase 1 (survey) of this project is comprised of 93 jailed fathers from the aforementioned sites, who volunteered for the study. Eighty-three of the fathers were housed at the large, urban jail and the remaining 10 were housed at the small, rural jail.

Instrument

The questionnaire for Phase I of the project was based on the questionnaire that was used in the pilot project for this study[3] (Hanrahan, et al, 1996; Martin, et al, 1995).

Despite some limitations, the questionnaire was a useful tool for collecting demographic data, and limited information about the inmates' social and family characteristics. Unfortunately, the questionnaire format was less successful at capturing the very complex nature of the phenomena that were the crux of the study, namely, the salience of the parental role and the perceptions of incarcerated fathers regarding their separation from their child (ren). It became clear that these issues would require dialogue between researcher and respondent.

---

[3] The pilot study was completed at a medium-security prison in Western Pennsylvania. A total of 105 inmates completed a self-administered questionnaire and a parenting inventory designed to assess the respondent's parental attitudes and behaviors (including maladaptive behaviors).

The revised questionnaire permitted the researcher to identify demographic information and family characteristics of the jailed fathers, collect limited information on their pre-incarceration parental relationships, and information on contact with family members during confinement. One of the goals of this project was to determine the ways in which the pre-incarceration parental relationships, and contact with family members during incarceration, influence the stress of the jail experience. It was theorized that separation from children is a stressor for fathers. Yet, it must be re-emphasized that this is not the only, and for some it is not the most severe, stressor faced in jail. Consequently the revised questionnaire includes measures of both the level of stress experienced in the jail environment, and the affective response to the stress.

Gibbs (1991) has suggested that each inmate in a jail setting has certain needs from their environment. For example, some inmates have a strong need for privacy, while other inmates may have a strong need for safety. Similarly, each environment provides variable levels of opportunities for satisfying these needs. When the environment meets an individual's needs, he/she will be at ease in that environment. However, if the environment does not meet an individual's needs, the person will be ill at ease, and he/she will experience stress (Gibbs, 1991).

It was necessary to be mindful that both separation from loved ones, and being housed in a county jail, have the capacity to cause stress. Thus, the questionnaire included versions of the Jail Preference Inventory and the Jail Environmental Quality Scale, which assess both the environmental needs of the inmate and the supply of those resources in the jail environment. This "supply-demand congruence model" was proposed by Gibbs (1991; 1987) and has been used with incarcerated parents (Lindquist and Lindquist, 1997).

The original Jail Preference Inventory (JPI) used a comparison-by-pairs format in which an item representing each dimension is paired, both positively and negatively, with an item representing every other dimension. The result was an "instrument with 84-item pairs in which each environmental dimension is measured by a 24-item need or demand scale that reflects the relative salience of the need" (Gibbs, 1991, p. 359).

The original Environmental Quality Scale (EQS) used by Gibbs (1991) was a 21-item scale that measured the perceived supply of the needed resource (dimension) in the environment. Gibbs (1987; 1991) conducted interviews with inmates at two points in time - within 72 hours of intake and a follow-up after 5 days of incarceration. The reliability coefficients for the JPI and the EQS for both administration periods (initial and follow-up) and the reliability coefficients were encouraging, ranging from .30 to .79 (Gibbs, 1991, p. 362).

In a later work, Gibbs and Hanrahan (1992) conducted a study with college students in which they used both short and long versions of the Environmental Preference Inventory (EPI), which is similar to the JPI, and short and long versions of the EQS. Gibbs and Hanrahan (1992) concluded that the scale correlations for the two versions of the EQS were "moderate to substantial" (p. 27).

The researcher for the current project was concerned about the respondents' ability and willingness to complete a lengthy questionnaire. Consequently, based on the success that Gibbs and Hanrahan (1992) had using shortened versions of the scales, it was decided that modified versions of the JPI and the EQS would be appropriate for this research project. These versions are outlined below.

Jail Preference Inventory

The "demand" instrument, the Jail Preference Inventory (JPI) developed by Gibbs (1991, p. 358) contains seven scales that measure the following dimensions:

Privacy: A preference for solitude, isolation, peace, and quiet; the absence of extreme noise and crowded situations.

Safety: A concern for personal physical safety; a preference for settings that reduce the likelihood of person-to-person confrontations.

Certainty: A preference for consistency, clarity, including consistent rules and procedures; a desire to reduce ambiguity in situations.

Assistance: A need for aid in handling problems; a desire to
receive help in completing tasks or obtaining services, either
within the institution or from other criminal justice or social
service agencies.

Support: A desire for empathetic, warm and understanding
interactions; a need for emotional support and help with
personal problems.

Activity: A need for stimulation in order to be occupied and fill
time; a need for distraction.

Autonomy: A desire to have control over one's life; preference for
freedom in making decisions.

According to Gibbs, the environmental dimensions "are based on
Toch's research with prison inmates, and some of the JPI items were
inspired by or adapted from other instruments which measure
environmental needs" (1991, p. 360).

This project utilized a shortened version of the JPI, consisting of
only the positive pairings. The result was an instrument with 42-item
pairs in which the respondent is forced to choose between the two
statements, as shown below.

Which would you prefer?

56) A housing unit where you have   A housing unit where you
have privacy   safety

64) Staff who allow you some privacy   Staff who are concerned a
                                           about your safety

Each dimension was matched with every other dimension on two
occasions in the questionnaire, and there are 12 items that correspond
to each dimension. When using this type of forced comparison, the
respondent has to choose between two items, or dimensions, both of
which may be desirable, as in the examples above. The result is a 12-
item demand scale that reflects the relative salience of each need. This
format permitted the researcher to determine which need was strongest,
or most salient, for each individual.

Environmental Quality Scale

The Environmental Quality Scale used for this project consisted of 7 statements that represent each of the aforementioned environmental dimensions. The statements were chosen by reviewing the item-total correlations from the follow-up administration of the EQS from Gibbs' 1991 study and selecting the single item that had the strongest item-total correlation. The statements were presented on a 10-centimeter line and respondents were asked to indicate how strongly they agreed or disagreed with each statement by placing a slash across the line. For example:

You can grab some time to yourself to think things through in here.

_____

Strongly   Strongly
disagree   agree

The result is a score between 1-10 that reflected the perceived supply of each environmental dimension in the jail.

Negative Affect Measure – Emotion Index

Stress is a difficult concept to define though most can describe it in personal terms. According to Cohen, Kesslar and Gordon (1995), stress can be thought of as a process in which "environmental demands tax or exceed the adaptive capacity of the organism, resulting in psychological and biological changes that may place the person at risk for disease" (p. 3). Using this definition, stress can be seen as "stimulus-response" event for individuals.

There are three components to the stress event: (1) environmental experiences – these are the environmental demands, stressors or events; (2) subjective evaluations of the stressfulness of the event – these are the individual appraisals or perceptions of stress; and (3) affective, behavioral, or biological responses to the stress event (Cohen, et al, 1995).

The first two components of the stress event were measured using the JPI and the EQS. Thus the final measure in the questionnaire was a negative affect measure because, "environmental demands that are appraised as stressful are generally thought to influence disease risk through negative emotional responses" (Cohen, et al, 1995, p. 18). It has been established previously that jail confinement is stressful, and that for most individuals, separation from family is stressful. It seems reasonable that these environmental demands will result in negative affective responses for most individuals. Previous research shed some light on the kind of affective responses that might be most common and those were depression, anxiety, and loneliness (Lanier, 1983; Rokach and Cripps, 1999). Additionally, Gibbs and Hanrahan (1992) incorporated a measure of negative affect in their study of college students. The researchers measured depression, loneliness, anxiety, and anger. Because of the overlap between the prior prison-based research findings and the Gibbs and Hanrahan (1992) measure, the researcher utilized this negative affect measure.

The respondents were asked to report how often they experienced each emotion or feeling, and then place a slash across a 10-centimeter line to indicate the frequency of each emotion as illustrated below.

How often do you experience **loneliness?**

Never   Always

The result is a score between 1-10 that reflected the relative frequency of the negative emotion. The scores for each of the four items (loneliness, anger, anxiety, and depression) were combined to form the "emotion index" (range of 0 – 40).

Procedures

The questionnaire was administered to groups ranging in size from 2-20. The researcher read the questionnaire aloud to each group of respondents. This method addressed the issue of literacy, which is a concern with incarcerated populations, and it also permitted the researcher to answer any questions that arose. Still, there were some men who answered the questionnaire at their own pace, and based on the completed surveys, there were several questions that some men did not understand and did not answer appropriately, or were unable to use the response format provided.

PHASE II – INTERVIEWS

Recruitment and Sampling

The sample for Phase II was comprised of individuals who had completed the questionnaire and indicated an interest in participating in face-to-face interviews by responding to the final question on the survey. For this phase, the researcher sampled from the pool of volunteers, based on their availability. A total of 26 interviews were completed, but one respondent inadvertently turned off his microphone. Thus, there are a total of 25 interview respondents.

Interview Protocol

A semi-structured interview protocol was used with each respondent. The purpose of the interviews was to explore with the fathers three broad areas: (1) their families of origin, which included their childhood relationships with their parents, and the way that these influenced the men's paternal behavior; (2) the salience or importance of their parenting roles, with a focus on their relationships with their children prior to incarceration; and (3) the impact of incarceration on their familial relationships, including their feelings about being separated from their children, the frequency and descriptions of contact with their children, and post-release expectations and plans.

Procedures

Information from the questionnaire was used to classify respondents as either "parents," men who (a) resided with all of their minor child during the six months prior to incarceration, or (b) had substantive (daily) contact with a minor child during the six months prior to incarceration, "biological fathers," men who did not reside with any of their children, or "mixed parents," men who resided with some of their children, but not all of them. "Parents" were in the minority (n = 17), and the "mixed parent" category was approximately the same size (n = 20). The "biological father" category was the largest (n = 46). Not all respondents fit into these categories. Five respondents had only adult children, four respondents reported that their children had been born during their incarceration, and one respondent failed to answer the items regarding the number of children and their living arrangements prior to incarceration.

The initial interviewing strategy was to first interview "parents" to allow the researcher to better understand the common characteristics and common concerns of these men before interviewing the next category of fathers. When these interviews were completed, the researcher planned to interview the "biological fathers" and the "mixed parents" on subsequent visits to be able to identify and understand similarities and differences across the groups. However, this sampling strategy was not always possible because of environmental constraints.

Obviously, these interviews were not occurring in a laboratory in which the researcher has a great deal of control, but in two jails. Hence, in this environment there is a rapidly diminishing sample. Because the researcher was granted access to "sentenced" housing units, the turnover was not as great as in other units in the jail (e.g. intake), but the decay of the sample was much greater than it would be in a prison. While the researcher anticipated some attrition, the decay rate exceeded expectations.

An additional note about the interviewing process is necessary. While some of the men appeared indifferent about completing the survey, nearly all of the men were eager to participate in an interview. There are likely several reasons for this. First, it may have been seen as a break from the monotony of the daily routine at the jail. Second, the men may have felt as if this were an opportunity to express concerns that they typically were not able to express. Parenting concerns are not frequently a focus in the jail environment and many of the men expressed that there should be a greater emphasis on the needs of parents. Third, the interviews represented an opportunity for the men to speak, on an individual basis, with a person who was interested in what they had to say. Again, it is unusual in the jail setting to participate in this type of communication. Finally, the researcher is a female. The housing units are obviously single gendered, and it is unusual to have contact with a female. It is possible that the inmates were interested in talking with the researcher simply because it gave them the opportunity to talk with someone of the opposite gender.

As a result, when the researcher arrived on the housing units, she was met by many men who were eagerly volunteering to be interviewed. The researcher was cognizant of the decay rate and aware that volunteers were crucial. If the preferred respondents were unavailable, and the researcher had refused to interview other volunteers, there was a possibility that the general willingness to participate would decline. For these reasons, it was necessary at times to deviate from the plan to interview a specific "kind" of father, and instead to interview those individuals who were willing and available on the days of data collection. Hence, if there were no "parents" available on a particular housing unit, but there were "fathers" who were available and requesting to be interviewed, the researcher decided to interview these men at that time. It is very unlikely that this modification to the original sampling strategy had any impact on the data. The final interview sample consisted of six "parents," seven "mixed parents," and twelve "biological fathers."

The researcher interviewed the respondents in a location designated by the jail administrators. The length of the interview varied significantly with one lasting 2 hours and another lasting only 35 minutes. Most of the interviews, however, were between 60-90 minutes. The respondent dictated the length of the interview, in large part. Each interview was audio taped to ensure accuracy and transcribed by a professional typist.

The researcher used a data management software package (QSR NUD*IST) during analysis of the qualitative data from the interviews.

SUBJECT PARTICIPATION AND PROTECTION

Phase I

This project focused on jailed fathers and special precautions were taken to insure that the individuals who participated in either phase of the study experienced no harm. First, it was stressed to all respondents that participation in this study was completely voluntary. The researcher clearly articulated that there were neither benefits nor rewards for participating, nor penalty for not participating. All participants were informed that they could choose to withdraw from participating in the project at any time and were instructed on how to do so.

All survey respondents were given a thorough overview of the research project and the researcher answered all questions that they had. They were asked to sign a consent form to indicate their willingness to participate, and they were given a copy of the consent form to keep. Any survey that did not have a signed consent form was not used. While it was not possible to guarantee anonymity, confidentiality was guaranteed. Each survey respondent was assigned a code number known only to the researcher. The consent forms were removed from the survey as soon as the master list of respondents was updated so that the completed questionnaires have no identifiers except for the confidential code number. The list of respondent code numbers was kept in a secure location for the duration of the project.

Phase II

Prior to the initiation of the interview, the respondents were told clearly that the interview was completely voluntary and that there were neither rewards for participating, nor penalty for not participating. The respondents were also told prior to the interview that they could decline answering any question that they felt uncomfortable with, or that they could choose to end the interview at any time. All participants were asked to sign a consent form to indicate their willingness to participate in the interview phase of the study and they were given a copy of the consent form to keep. Individuals who participated in the interview phase were identified using the code number from their respective surveys. Code number similarly identified the audiotapes of the interviews. During the interview itself, every attempt was made to avoid using the individual's first name. If the researcher referred to the respondent by name, this was removed during transcription. For example, if the respondent's name was Daniel, the transcribed material refers to him as "D." The tapes were transcribed as quickly as possible following the interview and the original tapes and transcribed interviews will be kept in a secure location until a time when they can be destroyed. Similarly, a master list of names has been kept throughout the duration of the project, and will be destroyed as soon as possible following the federal guidelines for research.

It was recognized that the topics of the interview session might cause emotional distress for some of the respondents. The researcher verified in advance, the availability of counseling personnel at each site and ascertained the procedure for initiating contact. Additionally, the researcher has experience in crisis intervention, mental health intakes and diagnosis, and counseling. While it was beyond the role of the researcher to counsel participants, this prior professional experience permitted the researcher to identify those participants who were in distress and in need of additional support. Throughout the duration of the project, there were no events that required referral to counselors.

CHAPTER 3

The Family of Origin
Examining the Roots of Paternal Behavior

"I cannot think of any need in childhood as strong as the need for a father's protection." Sigmund Freud (1931)

"Most human beings desire to have children and desire also that their children should grow up to be healthy, happy, and self-reliant. For those who succeed the rewards are great; but for those who have children but fail to rear them to be healthy, happy, and self-reliant the penalties...may be severe"
John Bowlby (1980)

When employing a multi-method approach, it may seem logical to provide the reader with results and findings from the first method, in this instance, the survey, and then to provide the findings from the second method, the interviews. In some instances, for example in outlining the demographic profile of the fathers, presenting the findings in this fashion makes the information more clear. However, for the most part, integration of the material better captures the findings from this study.

The chief argument for integration is that the information gathered from the surveys is often bolstered or clarified with the interview data. For example, about half of the men indicated on the survey that both parents had reared them during their childhood. However, during the interview, it became clear that this response category meant different things for different men. As an illustration of this, the following respondent is a 24-year old father of five. He indicated on the questionnaire that his mother and father reared him. However, upon interviewing him, it was evident that he meant merely that both parents were present in his life -- not that he was part of a stereotypical nuclear family.

> IER: When you were growing up, whom did you live with, for the most part?
>
> U28: I was really back and forth. For the most part, I lived with my mother though. Like I was my mother's child and my sister was my dad's child.
>
> IER: So you have a stepsister?
>
> U28: No, just my sister. Well, I have older brothers and sisters, but they are from different marriages. It was just my younger sister and I growing up.
>
> IER: Okay. So you said you lived with your mom for the most part. What about your sister?
>
> U28: She mostly lived with my dad. After my mom and dad broke up, she stayed mostly with my dad. Cause her and my mom didn't get along too good because my sister could get over on my dad.

Later in the interview, the researcher asked the respondent about the kinds of activities that he and his father participated in together.

> IER: What kinds of activities did you participate in with your parents?
>
> U28: My dad took me to a few baseball games. What else did my father and I do? I block a lot of it out because I used to be a class clown so I used to get my behind whooped. (Chuckles)

All the time. What else did my father and I do? We didn't really like play in the yard or nothing together. He used to take us for rides to get ice cream and stuff like that. Well, mainly my mom would take us for rides to get ice cream to get away from my dad because he would be in the house screaming, hollering, going crazy.

This young father reported on his survey that he had been reared by both of his parents. However, it was clear in speaking with him that he and his father did little together, and they did not reside in the same home for a good portion of the respondent's youth. The researcher assumed that if a respondent reported that he had been "reared by both parents" that this meant either he had lived with both parents, or both parents had played an integral role in the individual's childhood. This was not always the case. As Keith Crew points out, "one assumption of surveys, which seems so obvious that it is usually ignored, is that the researcher and the respondent are speaking the same language" (cited in Babbie, 1989, p. 246). However, this is often a faulty assumption, as words and phrases can mean different things to different individuals. The point that needs to be emphasized is that, while it is possible to report from the survey the percentages of respondents who fall in specific categories (e.g. the percent who reported they were reared by both parents, or the percent who reported they were reared by single parent) it is not possible to decipher from the survey data exactly what "reared by" means for these respondents.

The above respondent further indicated on his survey that he was not residing with any of his five children at the time of his arrest. Yet, during the interviews, he divulged that he was actually living with four of them. It is possible that some of the questions were difficult for the men to respond to, especially when they answered the questionnaire at their own pace. It became evident during the interviews that, while the researcher believed that the questions on the survey were straightforward, many times the response categories provided were unable to capture the complexity that was common in the lives of many respondents. Hence, to enhance clarity and understanding, it seems prudent to integrate the data from both phases of the study when possible and to use the interview data as a check on the validity of questionnaire responses.

PROFILE OF JAILED FATHERS

Analyses reported below are based on the self-reports of 93 inmate fathers jailed in two separate county jails. One hundred five surveys were administered but twelve were excluded for the following reasons: 3 of the respondents were not fathers; 4 respondents failed to answer 50% or more of the questions; 4 respondents chose to discontinue their participation; and 1 questionnaire was not returned. The final sample consisted of 93 jailed fathers, 83 from the large, urban jail and 10 from the small, rural jail. Twenty-six of the 93 jailed fathers were interviewed following completion of the questionnaire. One of the interviewees inadvertently turned off his microphone at the beginning of the interview, hence there is interview data from 25 respondents.

Demographics

Table 3 presents the demographic profile of the jailed fathers who participated in this study. The jailed fathers were for the most part either Black or White; the majority of respondents in this study were Black (63.4%, n = 59). The percentage of Black respondents in this study was somewhat higher than the urban jail average for the preceding year (56.5% - Allegheny County Jail Report, 1997). Thirty percent of the jailed fathers were White (n = 28), 2.2% were Latino (n = 2), and 2.2% were American Indian (n = 2). One respondent categorized himself as "Other," and one father did not classify himself. Because of the racial dichotomy that was present in the sample, the interviews were limited to Black and White fathers.

The average age of the jailed fathers in this study is 32 years. Nearly 85% (n = 79) of the fathers had at least a high school education. This is comparable to the national educational attainment average. In 1998, 88.1% of 25 to 29-year-olds had a high school education.

Table 3: Demographic Profile of Jailed Fathers

		All fathers (n = 93)	Rural (n = 10)	Urban (n = 83)	Interviewees (n = 26)
Average Age		**32.4**	**32.3**	**32.23**	**33.69**
Race					
	White	**n = 28** (30.1%)	**n = 7** (70%)	**n = 21** (25.3%)	**n = 9** (34.6%)
	Black	**n = 59** (63.4%)	**n = 2** (20%)	**n = 57** (68.7%)	**n = 16** (61.5%)
	Other	**n = 5** (5.4%)	**n = 1** (10%)	**n = 4** (4.8%)	**n =1** (3.8%)
	Missing	**n = 1** (1%)	-----	**n = 1** (1%)	----
Education					
	Less than HS	**n = 14** (15.1%)	**n = 3** (30%)	**n = 11** (13.3%)	-----
	HS Grad	**n = 44** (47.3%)	**n = 2** (20%)	**n = 42** (50.6%)	**n = 13** (50%)
	Post HS	**n = 35** (37.6%)	**n = 5** (50%)	**n = 30** (36.1%)	**n = 13** (50%)
Employment					
	Full-time	**n = 54** (54.1%)	**n = 7** (70%)	**n = 47** (56.6%)	**n = 13** (50%)
	Part-time	**n = 15** (16.1%)	**n = 1** (10%)	**n = 14** (16.9%)	**n = 4** (15.4%)
	Not Employed	**n = 22** (23.7%)	**n =2** (20%)	**n = 20** (24.1%)	**n = 8** (30.8%)
	Missing	**n = 2** (2%)	----	**n = 2** (2%)	----
Earnings					
	Under $10,000	**n = 32** (37.2%)	**n = 6** (60%)	**n = 26** (31.3%)	**n = 6** (23%)
	$10,001-$15,000	**n = 16** (17.2%)	**n = 1** (10%)	**n = 15** (18.1%)	**n = 5** (19.2%)
	$15,001-$25,000	**n = 20** (21.5%)	**n = 1** (10%)	**n = 19** (22.9%)	**n = 4** (15.4%)
	Over $25,000	**n = 18** (19.4%)	**n = 2** (20%)	**n = 16** (19.2%)	**n = 5** (19.2%)
	Missing	**n = 7** (7%)	----	**n = 7** (8%)	**n = 4** (15%)

Over one-third of the fathers (37.6%, n = 35) reported that they had at least some post-secondary education, which is lower than the national average of 65.6% (available online at http://nces.ed.gov/pubs99/condition99/Indicator-59.html). Finally, 15% (n = 14) of the fathers indicated that they had less than a high school education.

Nearly three-quarters of the jailed fathers held jobs prior to their incarceration; fifty-seven percent of the fathers were employed full-time, and 17.2% were employed part-time. Still, the respondents had an unemployment rate that was nearly six times the national average and four to six times the local average. Approximately 23% of the fathers were unemployed. This is much greater than the both the national unemployment average of 4.1% (available online at: http://stats.bls.gov/newsrels.htm), and the respective county unemployment averages, which, in October 1999 were as follows: 3.4% in the urban county and 5.0% in the rural county (available online at: http://www.lmi.state.pa.us/clep/labforce.asp).

A majority of the fathers (56%) reported earning $15,000 or less per year prior to incarceration, with 38% reporting earnings of $10,000 or less per year. Approximately 23% earned between $15,000 and $25,000 per year. Only 20% of the jailed fathers earned over $25,000 per year. Thus, both the rate of employment and the level of employment are quite low among respondents.

The fathers who participated in the interviews had a demographic profile quite similar to the total sample. While the subsample of interviewees appeared to be better educated than the entire sample, they had similar racial, employment and economic characteristics (See Table 3).

The jailed fathers had a varied criminal history, with 74.2% reporting that they had been convicted of two or more offenses. The fathers' offense categories ranged from property crimes and drug offenses to interpersonal crimes.

As shown in Table 4, the most common offense is possession of drugs – 53.8% of the fathers reported a conviction for this offense. Approximately 41% of the fathers reported that they had been convicted of theft, and 35% had a Receiving Stolen Property (RSP) or a Disorderly Conduct conviction.

As mentioned in Chapter III, two of the four pods at the large, urban jail to which the researcher was granted access were "program pods," which likely influenced the number of drug offenders in the sample. Also, the pods at the large, urban jail were lower security pods, which removed more violent offenders from the sample.

Table 4: Jailed Fathers' Reported Convictions

Property Offenses	Interpersonal Offenses	Drug Crimes	Other Offenses
Theft (40.9%)	Simple Assault (31.2%)	Possession (53.8%)	Disorderly Conduct (35.5%)
RSP (35.5%)	Robbery (15.1%)	DUI (17.2%)	
Burglary (18.3%)	Aggravated Assault (12.9%)		Failure to Appear (29.0%)
Writing Bad Checks (5.4%)	Terroristic Threats (9.7%)		All Other Offenses (21.5%)

Percentages do not equal 100% because of multiple convictions

As one might expect, with the multiple conviction rate being so high, the fathers reported that they had been incarcerated on more than one occasion, most often in a county jail. The fathers indicated that they had been jailed an average of 4.2 times, including their current incarceration. Unfortunately, most of the fathers did not report their current offense. This was probably due to the format of the question on the survey. The fathers were given a list of crimes and asked to check all that they had been convicted of, and the large majority of respondents completed this section. The fathers were further asked to circle their most current offense, but the majority did not do this. The researcher believes that requiring the jailed fathers to answer two questions on one set of responses created some confusion and thereby reduced the response rate to the second question. An alternative explanation is that the men chose not to respond to this particular question, which seems unlikely given their willingness to discuss quite personal matters during the interview.

FAMILY OF ORIGIN

The voyage to fatherhood begins not when a man discovers that his wife or girlfriend is pregnant, but much earlier in his life when he is a child. As a child, he observed his own mother and father, or in their absence, his caretakers, and learned how they responded to a wide variety of situations and how they interacted with each other and with their children. These behaviors and interactions are filed away as memories that the individual then refers to, as he becomes an adult and a father. As John Bowlby (1988) has pointed out, parenting behavior is influenced by "our experiences – experiences during childhood especially" (p. 5). One of the goals of this project then was to explore the experiences of the respondents in their families of origin.

While the jailed fathers in this study experienced a range of family situations as children, the majority reported that both parents had reared them. As can be seen in Table 5, Black and White fathers reported that both parents reared them. Fifty percent (n=14) of White fathers and 47.4% (n=27) of Black fathers stated that were reared by both parents.

Table 5: Jailed Fathers' Families of Origin

	All Respondents		*White Respondents*		*Black Respondents*	
	Frequency	Valid %	**Frequency**	Valid %	**Frequency**	Valid %
Mother and father	44	48.4	**14**	50	27	47.4
Mother only	**28**	30.8	**9**	32.1	**19**	33.3
Father only	**3**	3.3	**0**	0	**2**	3.5
Foster parents	**3**	3.3	**0**	0	**2**	3.5
Grandparents	**7**	7.7	**4**	14.3	**3**	5.3
Other relatives	**2**	2.2	**0**	0	**2**	3.5
Other	**4**	4.4	**1**	3.6	**2**	3.5
Missing	**2**	Missing	**0**	0	**2**	Missing
TOTAL	**93**	100.1	**28**	100	**59**	100

In addition, similar proportions of Black and White fathers reported that their mother reared them. Thirty-two percent of White fathers (n = 9) and 33% of Black fathers (n = 19) were reared by single mothers. Data from the U.S. Census Bureau were retrieved to compare the respondents' family situations to the national averages for the time period when the respondents were in their families of origin. The U.S. Census Bureau reports that in 1980, 79% of "family groups" with minor children were two-parent family groups, and 19% of "family groups" with minor children were one-parent groups maintained by the mother. However, when these 1980 national averages are broken down by race, 83% of the White "family groups" with minor children were two-parent family groups, and the mother maintained only 15% of White "family groups." However, among Black "family groups," 48% were two-parent family groups and 49% were family groups maintained by the mother (available online at: http://www.census.gov/prod/ 99pubs/ 99statab/sec01.pdf).

In the current study approximately one-third of both White and Black respondents were reared by their mother only. According to the U.S. Census Bureau, both groups in the current sample are atypical in opposite directions. Because of the language of question 10 (who were you reared by), and the aforementioned problems in interpreting the responses, these findings are cautionary as the researcher is comparing Census Bureau data on family structure with the respondents perceptions on who was responsible for raising them. Still, it must be reemphasized that children reared in single parent homes maintained by the mother face greater hardships than do children reared in two-parent homes (Wilson, 1996).

The men who participated in the interviews confirmed that the dual parent family was most typical. Thirteen of the 25 (52%) respondents interviewed reported that both parents had reared them, and this meant that they were part of a nuclear family. As might be expected, the men reported both happy and troublesome memories of their childhoods, regardless of their family structure. Some of the men reported that they had fairly positive childhood experiences.

IER: Could you describe a typical day when you were growing up?

U33: Typical day growing up... Mostly I'd have a few friends. We'd always either ride bikes, skateboards. There was like this field about a mile away from my father's house, we'd go and they had a lot of fruit trees there. We basically go and pick apples and peaches and stuff like that. Then we'd end up eating them there and then we'd more less throw them at each other and stuff like. Pretty neat. We did a lot of bike riding, adventurous stuff. Go around anywhere we could find trees or whatever. Climb trees and stuff like that.

U29:   When I was young, before I was like eleven, twelve years old, (mumbles) wake up in the morning, go to school. Wake up in the morning, get dressed, go in the room and let my mom see what I'm dressed like (chuckles) then go to school, come home. Tell me to do my homework before I could go outside. Do that, or fake it. Fake like I'm doing it (chuckles). Eat dinner. Dinner was always ready early. Go outside, come in the house. I think my curfew was about 8:00. 8:00, 9:00 come in the house, take a bath, watch TV till I got ready to go to bed. Went to bed probably about 11:00, 10:30 or 11:00. Get ready for school the next day.

U32: It was fun. Played football, I had a lot of friends. We played football, we played games. Ate good everyday. Was clean everyday. We weren't rich. We wasn't poor either. It was good. It was good growing up. My mother did the best she could

The first respondent lived with both parents, the second lived with his mother, and the third respondent was reared by his mother, grandfather and aunts. Other respondents, however, had less positive experiences as children. Both of the following respondents reported living with both mother and father.

U39:   A typical day? Probably be getting into some kind of trouble, you know. Getting yelled at or something. That was probably a pretty typical day. Where I'd do something and get in trouble for it, get yelled at. Or get a spanking, or you know, get my ass beat or something. But I wasn't always getting an ass beating; it was more often getting punished, getting grounded or something like that.

U79: A lot of what I remember, to tell you the truth, other than not being at home was being with one of my brothers and sisters. They say that my older sister Mary, there used to be a joke in my house, where she was my mother because I was always with her most of the time and her kids. I have nieces that are only a couple of years younger than me. I guess you could pretty much say that I was raised by both mother and my sister.

Hence, the structure of the family does not appear to be the major determinant on the atmosphere in which the respondents were reared.

The jailed fathers were also queried about discipline. Historically, fathers have been viewed as the disciplinarian of the family. Many children have heard the retort, "wait until your father gets home." To better understand this issue, the jailed fathers were asked, "as a child, who was primarily responsible for disciplining you and your siblings?" Their responses are reported in Table 6.

Considering that both White and Black respondents reported being reared by both of their parents, it was expected that there would be similarity in the jailed fathers' reports of the primary disciplinarian. As outlined in Table 6, both White and Black fathers reported that their parents shared the responsibility of discipline in their families. Fifty percent (n = 14) of White fathers indicated that both their mothers and fathers were involved in their discipline. Among Black respondents, 42.9% (n = 24) reported being disciplined by both parents, and 44.6% (n = 25) of the indicated that their mothers were responsible for their discipline.

Also of interest is that, among this sample, the stereotypical "father as primary disciplinarian" of the family was not supported. Only four respondents, 2 White and 2 Black, indicated that their father was the individual most responsible for their discipline. Not surprisingly, it appears as though the inmates' reports regarding primary disciplinarian closely mirror their reported family structure (see Table 5).

Table 6: Individuals who Disciplined Jailed Fathers as Children

	All Respondents		White Respondents		Black Respondents	
	Frequency	Valid %	Frequency	Valid %	Frequency	Valid %
Mother and father	40	44.4	14	50	24	42.9
Mother only	32	35.6	6	21.4	25	44.6
Father only	5	5.6	2	7.1	2	3.6
Foster parents	1	1.1	0	0	1	1.8
Grandparents	8	8.9	5	17.9	3	5.4
Other relatives	1	1.1	0	0	1	1.8
Stepparents	1	1.1	1	3.6	0	0
Other	2	2.2	0	0	0	0
Missing	3	Missing	0	Missing	3	Missing
TOTAL	93	100	28	100	59	100.1

Intergenerational Incarceration

Researchers have suggested that children who have experienced enduring trauma in their lives (such as parental crime, arrest and incarceration) are at increased risk for engaging in maladaptive behaviors. "The long term outcome of most maladaptive coping mechanisms is delinquency or adult crime" (Johnston, 1995, p.80). The jailed fathers were asked both in the questionnaire and during the interviews if any of their family members, particularly their parents, were incarcerated. A total of twelve men (13%) reported on the questionnaire that their father had been incarcerated and one of these individuals reported that his mother had been incarcerated as well.

In the interview sample, two respondents indicated on their questionnaires that their father had been incarcerated and not a single respondent reported that their mother had been incarcerated. However, during the interview, four of 25 reported that their father had been incarcerated and one reported his mother had been jailed around the time of his birth. Hence, 20% of the interview respondents reported that a parent had been incarcerated. While the respondents recalled this aspect of their family life during the interviews, they seemed reluctant to discuss in great detail their parents' incarceration.

> IER: Were any of your family members ever in trouble with the law, ever incarcerated?
>
> U23: My father.
>
> IER: Is this when you were growing up.
>
> U23: Well first of all my father, I remember my father when I was I guess when I was five and younger. During past that time he was incarcerated and I didn't see my father any more until I was in my mid-twenties. So that was the extent of that.

The next respondent reported that his father also had spent time in a jail and, in fact, had died in prison. He spoke about what it was like to visit his father at a county jail.

> IER: Were any of your family members every in trouble or incarcerated?
>
> U28: My father.
>
> IER: Okay. How old were you?
>
> U28: I was about maybe 10 or 11. My dad was in…he was in for a couple times but he never did any major time until like around '95. He got 5 to 10 in the penitentiary for aggravated assault. He crashed a bus. He hit a lady in the process of that. All that stuff added up.
>
> IER: When he was incarcerated, when you were younger, did you ever visit him?

U28: Once.

IER: Do you have any recollection of what that was like?

U28: It was at the old county jail. All you could see was through the little window like at. I didn't like it. I told my mom I wanted to leave. And they let me go back outside and I sat down cause I didn't understand it. She had to explain it to me.

IER: What was that whole process like? Because as I'm going into the jail here, I have an idea of how the visitors are brought into the jail. Was it a similar situation at the old jail?

U28: I've never came here to visit. But at the old jail, it was weird. You went up the steps and you went into this gate and then back into this one room, through the room and when you came through the room on the other side of the door was like a big piece of metal separating everything with windows in it. The phone...you had to pick up the phone and talk like on some of these pods here.

IER: So not a pleasant experience?

U28: No. I didn't like it at all. Especially because you had to talk on the phone and you couldn't touch them, so.

IER: How did it make you feel?

U28: Hurts. Pain. It's just like you're dreaming. Like you're talking to him in a dream or something.

The interview data seem to suggest that respondents may have underreported the extent of parental incarceration on the questionnaire, and the interviewees' reluctance to discuss this information suggests that this is a sensitive issue for them.

Additionally, nine other interview respondents (36%) indicated that a sibling had been incarcerated and one respondent reported that one of his adult sons had been incarcerated. Thus, 60% of the interview respondents reported the incarceration of an immediate family member. The data from the interviews suggest that many of the respondents have experienced, personally, the impact of separation from loved ones due to incarceration.

Father-Son Relationship

There has been growing awareness and discourse on the important role that the father plays in the life of his children (Lamb, 1981; Robinson and Barrett, 1986; Marsiglio, 1995; Pitts, 1999). Along with this growing awareness of the significant role that a father plays, there is a simultaneous acknowledgment that not all men are willing or able to fulfill their paternal role or obligation (Furstenberg, 1995; Pitts, 1999). Consequently, one of the focuses of this study is to better understand the relationships that the jailed fathers had with their parents as they were growing up. Special emphasis was placed on exploring the father-child relationship that these men had.

While some of the men spoke lovingly of their fathers and described them in warm terms, others spoke of their fathers with hatred and anger as they recalled unpleasant childhood experiences.

The paternal model to which the jailed fathers had been exposed during their childhood ranged from the very positive to the very negative. A typology was developed to describe the paternal models that the jailed fathers experienced as children. The "Paternal Typology" is shown in Table 7. It includes both positive and negative paternal models as characterized by the interview respondents. This typology was developed as a means to capture the five themes that emerged during the analysis of the interview data.

Some of the jailed fathers characterized their father as falling into two categories (e.g. Alcoholic and Abusive). In these situations, the most salient characteristic, as recalled by the respondent, was used to categorize his father.

Table 7: Paternal Typology

Paternal Models	Characteristics
Positive Model	
"Loving and Emotionally Supportive"	These fathers were (1) present for their children; (2) supportive of their children; and (3) loving towards their children.
Positive/Negative Model	
"Financially Supportive"	The interviewees characterized these fathers as "workaholics." These fathers typically worked two jobs and provided financial support for their families but were absent during much of the interviewees' childhoods.
Negative Models	
"Absent"	These fathers were not present for much of the interviewees' childhood. Some of the absent fathers helped support their children and some did not. Some maintained contact and some did not. Interestingly, the jailed fathers frequently justified the absence of these parents and fantasized a stronger relationship than was present.
"Abusive"	These fathers were either (1) physically abusive, or (2) mentally abusive, or (3) both.
"Addicted"	These fathers were addicted to alcohol. These fathers were present, and were described as supportive. These men were described as "functional alcoholics."

The positive paternal model can be described as "Loving and Supportive." These fathers were: (1) present for their children; (2) supportive of their children; and (3) loving towards their children. A total of five respondents had fathers who were "loving and supportive." The respondent below describes the "Loving and Supportive" paternal model.

IER: Could you describe your parents to me?

U37: Sure. My dad is tough. He just recently passed away in October. He was 79. He was a very compassionate man, he was a caring man. He was very patient. He was a very loving father. Real "head of the household." He had a good job. He was a superintendent of the foundry [where he was employed]. He was a really great dad. He was busy a lot when we were young but he was a real good dad. (Continues to describe his mother).

IER: What about a typical day when you were growing up?

U37: A typical day would be I would get up and go to school. Come home and eat and go out and play with my friends. When I was young that is what I remember. Just going outside and playing a lot with my friends. Coming in, doing my homework, watching TV and going to bed. My dad was involved in a lot, he was getting his degree. He had a master's in education. He was in Toastmasters and he was in the PTA. But he always wanted to help me with my homework. So that was like a typical day.

The following respondent also described the "loving and supportive" paternal model.

IER: If you had to choose five words to describe your dad, what words would you choose?

R11: Hard-working, a good father. He provided for us all when we were growing up. My mother the same way. A very good mother. We got everything that we wanted the whole way up. I mean we were raised properly. The way we should be raised.

IER: What other words would you use to describe your dad.

R11: Other words...he's just a go-getter. Always got to be doing something. Never stays still. Just continually do something. That's basically how I could sum it up anyway. He just, my father loves to work and now he just finally retired. But as soon as he gets off work he gets in the yard and mows the lawn and does this and does that. We kind of try and follow in his footsteps but along the way things happen. But what can you do, so.

IER: What kinds of activities did you participate in with your parents as you were growing up?

R11: Vacations. Lot of fishing trips. Lot of amusement parks. Camping. Things of that nature.

IER: Did your dad like the outdoors or did mom or both?

R11: Both. They both loved the outdoors. Basically that's all they do now is camp. That's really about all we did. Growing up dad always had us out there working in the yard when he was first putting up his house. Tried to work us to death but other than that. Basically every time we wanted to go somewhere, we'd name a specific place and he'd take us. There was really no problem there.

Not every individual had a positive paternal role model. While each individual had his own story to tell, there were themes that emerged from these more negative accounts. While it was not one focuses of this study to examine race as it related to parenting style, a race-related pattern did seem to emerge in the analysis of the interview data. Black interview respondents were more likely than White interview respondents to have had "Absent" fathers. Conversely, the

White interview respondents were more likely to have experienced "Workaholic," "Abusive," or "Addicted" fathers (See Table 8).

Table 8: Paternal Typology by Race

Paternal Models	African-American	White	Other
"Loving and Supportive"	n = 3	n = 2	--
"Workaholic"	n = 1	n = 3	--
"Absent"	n = 9	--	n = 1
"Abusive"	n = 1	n = 2	--
"Addicted"	n = 1	n = 2	--

As race was not intended to be an independent variable in this study, and was therefore not considered in the sampling methodology, further analysis of the relationships involving race would not be appropriate at this time. Further, as suggested in Chapter 1, the impact of race cannot be properly viewed outside of a broader "macro-structural" context.

Four of the respondents had fathers who were rarely around because of demands from work. While these men provided for their families, and provided a "role model" of a working father, the respondents seemed to resent not having more time with their fathers. The following respondent is a 42-year old father of two. He is the oldest of ten children. The researcher asked him to describe his parents.

IER: Okay. Could you describe your parents to me?

U36: [Respondent first described mother]. My dad is dead. He died when he was 61 of a heart attack. He always worked two jobs. I have a lot of hurt because me and him...I was the oldest boy and I started drinking right out of high school, or grade school, going into ninth grade. I didn't see things the way that I see them now. When I was a kid I had blinders on. I only saw things the way I wanted to see them. Not the big picture. My dad and me we would argue a lot. Couple times it got physical. I always resented some things that he did and didn't do.

IER: Such as?

U36: I was a pretty good baseball player and my dad was working all the...he left at 6:30 in the morning. He went to the mill. He didn't get done there until 3:00 and he had to be at another job at 4:00 and work till 12:00. But I was blind to the thought that he had to do this for us to have clothes and eat. There were ten of us. He had a house payment and bills, food bills, clothing, school. My mother couldn't work because she had all the kids. How could she do anything. I didn't see it then. But now I realize what a great, good man he was. But I didn't see it then. He didn't have time to come and watch me play. I blew up one day and I was crying. I told him, "I hate you. You don't even have time to come see me play." The only days he was off was Sunday. It was his only day off. Couple of times I seen him after all that happened, I was on a pony league traveling type baseball team and I seen him up in the back of the stands a couple of games. He had to sneak out of work to do that. I guess I got my point across because my younger brothers whenever they had a basketball game or baseball game, he did anything he could to go so that he didn't make that same mistake. But you don't see these things till...You think back to what your dad had to give up for you and your brothers and your sisters and his wife and you hurt inside because all the problems you caused him, you know. Growing up with those blinders...because I was young. I didn't see the whole picture.

As this respondent expressed, his perspective changed with age and he realized the sacrifice that his father had made in order to support his family. However, he seemed intent on not behaving the same way with his son, even though he described himself as a hard-worker who is not able to sit still. While the respondent and his wife were separated, the respondent saw his son daily, and reported that they spent a lot of time playing.

> U36: As soon as he came home from school he was, "dad." If I wasn't home [from work] yet, as soon as I got home we had a deal. You call me, I call you. See where I live it's a neighborhood loaded with kids. As soon as [his son] would get there, all the kids would seem to because I would get games together. We'd play "hide and seek", "release the ?", pick-up football game, kickball. Everyday I had something and we had a gang of kids there. Sometimes [his son] would even get mad because it wasn't enough me and him just. We couldn't catch football just me and him. As soon as we went out to start...I didn't mind because a lot of the kids didn't have a dad in the neighborhood. They are single parent mom and they needed an older person to play with. I had time. I quit drinking almost two years ago and I have time.

This respondent reported interacting with his son in a way that he wished he and his father had.

> U36: My dad was from the old school. My dad never hugged me. There is not a day that I'm with my son that I won't hug him. Because I wanted my dad to hug me. I really did. But he never did. One time I said to him, "dad you never even told me that you love me." We were fighting. He said, "you know 'we' love you." But it taught me something. Now I've come to realize that my dad was from the old school. You just didn't do it.

The above respondent longed to have his father show affection and spend time with him when he was a child. As a result of his unfulfilled wish, he made attempts to develop a relationship with his son that included what the respondent missed as a child.

Other men with "workaholic" fathers reported that they had been able to spend time during their youth with their fathers by working with them. The following respondent expressed this during his interview.

IER: Could you describe your parents to me?

U38: They were normal I guess. My dad worked two jobs. My mom was a home keeper and stayed home and cleaned house and stuff like that. My dad died when I was 19 and she went to work in the steel mill and stuff. But other than that, it was sort of the normal all American growing up. My dad was painting contractor that was one of the jobs he had. I went to work when I was 11 years old. I still went to school but when everybody else had days off and vacation and stuff I was making jack. Other than that though like I said, the family was normal. Nobody was ever in trouble. That kind of stuff. Where I went wrong, I don't know.

IER: If you had to choose five words to describe your father?

U38: Friendly, strict, hard working. Is that one word?

IER: Yes.

U38: Conscientious and I'm thinking of a word that means...he was real like, everything he did had to be just right. Like on the paint jobs. I don't know what word would describe that.

IER: Perfectionist?

U38: Yeah. That's a good one. (Laughs) Thank you.

IER: When you were growing up, what kinds of activities did you participate in with your parents?

U38: With my dad I worked a lot. They belonged to the Elks in [names town], they had the Elks swimming pool when I was growing up until I got a little older and went my own way. Went on some vacations. Lot of family picnics, family dinners, stuff like that. Sunday dinners, holiday dinners. Close family. I mean family, family.

IER: With your dad, what did you do?

U38: My dad, like I say, I went to work when I was 11 years old. I started working with him. My dad was basically a workaholic. He worked in the mill. He worked steady 3 to 11 in the mill and he'd run his paint crew on the outside and on weekends and stuff. So basically with my dad I worked a lot.

IER: You spent a lot of time with him though?

U38: Yeah.

IER: How close were you to your dad?

U38: I was pretty close. Growing up, especially when I hit my teenage years we'd butt heads a lot. But basically I was pretty close to him. I worked with him all the time. My dad was a down to earth type guy. He had a lot of friends.

For this respondent, spending time with his father meant working with him, yet this allowed him be with his father and interact with him. Through these kinds of interactions, and by observing his parents, the respondent learned what a father should do for his children.

IER: Generally speaking, what do you think are the three most important things that a father does for his children?

U38: All the things that I don't do. Ahhh...financial support, moral support and guidance.

IER: Did your dad do these things for you?

U38: Yeah.

The respondent reported that he had not done a very good job of parenting his son, who was 19 years old.

> IER: Now think about all of these things that your parents did as you were growing up, the financial support, the understanding, taking care of you and all of the things you listed. Now think about yourself as a parent. How have you as a father been influenced by the things that your mom and dad did?

> U38: The way I act as a parent, probably not too much by what my parents did. My parents never acted like I do, I know that. They always tell me that I'm the black sheep of the family. The prodigal son, you know. I have my moments where I'm straight and I've "A #1" on my family's list. Then I have moments like now when they don't even like to talk to me.

> IER: But did your parents influence you?

> U38: Yeah. I know what I'm supposed to do. I understand what I'm supposed to do (laughs). It kind of gets screwed up in the translation sometimes though.

This respondent could identify that his parents, and his father in particular, had influenced him, and had provided a role model of paternal behavior. In this particular situation, the respondent's addiction seemed to interfere with his ability to be the kind of parent that his father was.

Other men (n=10) had "Absent" fathers. For these men, there was no "dad" to look up to or to interact with. The following respondent reported living with his mother, grandfather, and aunts. The researcher was curious about his relationship with his father.

> IER: What about your dad? Did you ever have contact with your dad when you were growing up?

U32: Yeah, not that much though.

IER: About how much? How often did you see him?

U32: I didn't see him a lot. That might be the one thing I have a problem with. But I didn't see my father when I was younger growing up. He was in the service. I never seen him that much. Maybe once a year or something like that. I really didn't see him a lot.

IER: Okay, so you didn't really spend time with him or interact with him.

U32: Nope.

IER: [First asked respondent to describe his mother, which he did]. Is it possible for you to describe your father?

U32: He was all right. Just didn't take care of his responsibilities. I feel like one of my reasons for going on the road that I took was because I didn't have no fatherly guidance. My grandfather, he could only do so much because he was crippled and he was older. He was older, but my dad, describe him? He was irresponsible and that's the way I've become. He was irresponsible and he tried to come into my life now and tries to be a father as far as like correcting me for my wrong doings and I have a problem with that. Because he didn't correct me when I was younger. But I am trying to establish a relationship with him now. Before I came to jail I would call him and stuff but he never called me back. So I ain't...I just made my mind up I'm not going to make the effort no more to contact him unless he try and contact me. Because I'm always the one trying to reach out but he never...he don't meet me half way.

This same respondent later broke down in tears during the interview when talking again about how little influence his father had on him. His words seemed to emphasize the truth for him; he missed having a father around when he was young and he was desperate for a relationship with his father at the present. The "Absent" paternal model seems to result in a consistent outcome. The son of an absent father seems to have a void in his life that he perhaps cannot quite capture in words, but is represented in his actions, especially when he becomes a father. This respondent who had tearfully recounted the lack of contact with his own father, acknowledged that he had followed in his father's footsteps in terms of parenting his own children.

> IER: You told me earlier that the most important things a father does are provide for his children, teach them responsibility, by actually showing them....
>
> U32: I didn't do that.
>
> IER:...and love them.
>
> U32: I loved them but I didn't show it so I really didn't love them. When they were first growing up I was there but as my drug addiction progressed, I wasn't there no more. I haven't set a good example for them within the past couple years. That hurts, too. I'm going to try to do something different when I get out. I really don't know how they feel about...well I think they still love me. As a matter of fact, I'm sure they love me. It's just my actions. My actions hurt them. I'm coming to grips with that. I don't want to do the same thing my father did to me. I don't want to do that to them and that's what happened so far, you know? I'm aware of that. I've been aware of it but I still didn't do nothing about it. But I'm aware of it. I'm really aware of it now.

This individual could identify what a father should do, yet he seemed unsure of how to actually do those things, and uncertain if he was capable. The above respondent seemed resentful of his father's absence. While not all of the individuals voiced resentment, the void that is left when the father was absent seemed to exist for all of the respondents, and if it did not show in their descriptions, it seemed present in their actions.

The next respondent described living with his older brother and sister-in-law as he was growing up. He was the youngest of eight children. His mother had passed away when the respondent was one and his father had apparently left him to be reared by older siblings. The respondent described his living situation.

U03: My dad didn't actually focus in the picture until I was like maybe seven. He was always there, provided for me and my sister, my youngest sister but he was with someone else. But he always provided for us. From what I remember, I was with my brothers or my sisters. That I can remember.

The respondent further indicated that, while he was certain that his father loved him, his father had not done the other things that this respondent felt a father should do for his children (e.g. setting an example for them and teaching them how to set goals for themselves). Still, this individual did not fault his father, nor did he seem to have any resentment toward him. The researcher asked the respondent to rate his father's performance.

IER: If you had to rate your dad on those three things, on a scale of one to ten, what would you give your dad?

U03: On the three things that I've mentioned, far as I know he would get a ten for loving me. My dad loved me very much. As far as setting goals, I would have to give him...he'd get half of that, a five. Because he wasn't really there. Middle school, grade school, he wasn't really there. I was moving around from house to house, from sisters to brothers. All around the city. What was the last one?

IER: You said setting an example.

U03: Yeah, educating. As far as educating me, like I said, he wasn't really there. I'd have to rate him like a five or a four.

IER: If you had to give him one composite score?

U03: As far as my dad? An eight. Because I know that he loved me but if he was there for me he would have been able to do these things. That's where I come out because I really loved my dad regardless of what he wasn't there for. I still loved my dad.

The score that this respondent gave his father seemed to reflect his wish that his father had been more involved than he was. Again, this individual seemed to follow in the footsteps of his father, as he became a parent. He reported having three children, ages 10, 15 and 17, with whom he did not reside, but kept in touch with via telephone. The researcher asked the respondent about his relationship with his children.

IER: How often were you seeing them [your children]?

U03: When I was out there I seen them maybe every two weeks. Whatever. But I talked to them like every other day on the phone. I was with them but I didn't live with them but I was with them. They know how to call me, they know how to page me or things like that.

IER: Is it kind of like your dad? The way your dad was with you?

U03: Yeah, sort of. But in a way not really, because my dad didn't really call me as much as I called him. I call them about everything. What's going on with them. I just want to know. He's ready to go to college, [oldest son] is ready to go to college. I got a stack of letters in there from him, you know what I'm saying....

The following respondent is a 23-year-old father with three daughters, by three different women. He had very limited contact with his natural father, seeing him for the last time when he was approximately 14 years of age.

IER: Can you describe your father to me?

U29: He was a good dude. He took care of me whenever I needed something. Whenever me and my mom called him and told him that I needed something. He took care of me. He used to come get me a lot. This is when I was staying in Alabama because I'm originally from Alabama. I used to go stay with him for the weekends or weeks or whatever. That was when him and my mom wasn't together. Then me and my mom moved back to [names city] and he moved back too. About three months after we moved back, he moved. He and my mom got back together. They was together for about a year, maybe a year and a half; split up again and he then he moved back to Alabama and that's where he's been ever since.

IER: So have you had any contact with him?

U29: Last time I was with him was '91. We went down to Alabama for a family reunion. That was the last time I had physical contact with him, like been with him. After that it was just like I started getting locked up in juvenile facilities and on and off and I never really made it back. He just died in March this year.

IER: If you had to come up with five words to describe your dad?

U29: He was responsible. He was an alcoholic, he drunk a lot. He was loving, caring and that's about it.

IER: How close were you to your dad?

U29: My dad was real cool even though in later years I hadn't seen him in about 8, 9 years. But I still used to talk to him on the phone. I meant to go down and see him. As a matter of fact, before I came here I had tickets. I was headed down there. I ended up with some warrants and ended up in here so I never got to see him again. We was cool. We was real cool. After I grew up, we really like, bonded. But we wasn't never together after I grew up. Just telephone conversations and stuff like that.

This young father seemed to have no anger or hostility toward his father and, in fact, indicated that he had done a fairly good job of parenting him. This individual reported that the three most important things a father does for his children are: (1) spends time with them, (2) provides financially for them, and (3) conveys his love for them. The researcher asked the respondent if his father had done those things for him.

> IER: What about if you had to rate your dad's performance on those three items on a scale of one to ten? What would you give him?

> U29: I'd give him an eight. As far as I when I was coming up all the way up until the time he moved back down to Alabama, I'd give him about an eight.

> IER: What about after that?

> U29: After that like I said, contact was gone. I called him like one time. After that I was into my thing. I was selling drugs and stuff so I didn't need him no more as far as like taking care of me or whatever. I think I called him like one time around Christmas. And he sent me some money up for Christmas. Other than that, I never really needed him. As far as that. As far as spending time, he was down there and I was up here so we couldn't do that. I know that he still loved me though. Whenever I would get into a jam and ended up in one of them juvenile facilities, my mom let him know. He'd send word through her to me telling me something. He was way down there. What could he tell me from down there for real.

Again, this young father seemed to take his cue about being a father from his father.

IER: So again, if you think of things that your parents did and now think of yourself as a father. How have you, as a father, been influenced by your parents?

U29: Only thing I can say on that one is make sure they have whatever they need. And me, I make sure that they have whatever they want too. If they ask me for something, they got it. I send somebody to get it for me. As far as like the time, my youngest baby, I spent more time with her than I probably have with both of my oldest daughters. My youngest baby, she's a year now. She was four months before I left. So you can imagine that. I spent more time with her in four months than I probably did with both of my oldest daughters which are 4. But I make sure they all have whatever they needed. If they ask me for something, whatever they wanted. As far as like time, taking them...I took them to the store. As far as like taking them to the park or letting them run around or whatever... What I called spending time was going over picking them up bringing them over my house and leaving them with my girl while I'm out running the streets and handling my business and doing my thing all the time. Or when I was still staying with my mom, going over and getting them and bringing them home and them staying there with my mom. When I come in at night, I spend some time with them. As far as like everyday, I'm always gone. I come in, bring them something or whatever but other than that, I'm always gone. I checked that since I've been here too.

IER: So you didn't do as good a job at spending time with them as you want to.

U29: Yeah.

Interestingly, these men conveyed that while they had room for improvement in their parenting, they were doing a better job than their fathers had done. Compared to their own fathers, they were better parents. Furthermore, it is possible that one of the reasons that the majority of respondents with absent fathers held little resentment toward them is because they have followed suit with their children. Perhaps through justifying their fathers' absence, and using their behavior as a referent for their own, these men can convince themselves that their children will be okay.

While the Absent-Father model seemed to result in the men having "missing pieces" (Pitts, Jr., 1999) as fathers, it was not the only negative paternal model to which the respondents were exposed. The Abusive-Father, while present in the household, interacts with his children in ways that result in psychic wounds. Three of the respondents identified this paternal type.

The first respondent is a 40-year old father of five children and four stepchildren. He resided with his third wife and 7 children (3 biological and 4 step) prior to his incarceration. He described a childhood that was filled with violence and terror. The researcher had asked the respondent to describe his parents, and the respondent began recounting his father's abusiveness.

> R03: It was really bad. I was thrown through the walls and end up in another room. Stuffed my head to the bottom of a pool till I turned blue. He knocked me out of a tree with a brick. He punched me so bad he carried me down the street. He thought I was dead. I was unconscious. I didn't dare open my eyes. I was bleeding so bad cause I knew if I did he would beat me again. He hit me with a car, a ton of things. I got beat with three yardsticks taped together with duct tape. It wasn't just one. Both [mother and father] of them were alcoholics. That was really rough. I guess, I'm not saying that what happened when I was a kid did this to me now. This is my own fault. I haven't been in trouble for like eight years and then this happened. It was my own fault.

The respondent described his mother as "a chicken" who was afraid of her husband and did nothing to protect her children.

> IER: [Did her behavior] Make you angry?

> R03: Yes. I was always mad at her because she let him do it to us. A lot of times we would just get a beating for no reason.

If I was bad and I would get a beating from my grandfather. He would whack me on my behind, that's okay. I deserved it. I'd go home. I would be sleeping in my bed and my father would come home. Here it is one o'clock, two o'clock in the morning and he would just start on us. "Your room's dirty," and he would yank us out of bed and start beating on us. Jesus Christ, I'm sound asleep what the heck do I know, you know. I'm only like nine, ten years old.

IER: Trying to figure out...

R03: Yeah, what did I do? I wasn't that bad, you know. But to him it was just a fiasco.

This respondent reported that the three most important things that a father does for his children are (1) love them, (2) protect them, and (3) provide for them.

IER: And how many of these things did your dad do for you?

R03: Christ. None. He never loved any of us. If we got into a fight out there and something happened, "you got yourself in it, get yourself out." Or my father, if I was getting in a fight with somebody, he'd tell me, "are you going to stand there or are you going to fight?" "And if you get beat, I'm going to beat you again." Providing, heh, I had a roof over my head. In those days we didn't have too much to eat, though. And there were days we never went to school because he wouldn't let us because we had bruises on us and he was hiding it. So how I ever made it through high school is beyond me I can tell you. Mainly, because of my grandmother. She was teaching on weekends. They allowed her to do this even when my father kind of put me I the hospital. He kicked me between the legs one time when I was thirteen years. Raised a testicle up so high that it almost exploded in me. And I had to have it lowered back down with traction and everything and my grandmother told the school she would tutor me. My mother brought me to my grandmother's house. I stayed there for two months. It only took two weeks before this thing healed. She kept me there for two months. She said, "this is the only way you're going to get out of this school year; if I tutor you enough and get your grades up high enough." So I stayed there with her. He really didn't help us at all. Not very much at all.

The researcher was interested in understanding what, if anything, the respondent had learned from his father about being a parent.

IER: If you think about your dad, what do you think are the most important things you learned from him about being a parent?

R03: Never strike your child. There is no reason. A child can't take that. You're talking about a person my size hitting on a kid that doesn't come to your ankle or your knee or your hip. And the force that you have when you get in a fight with a full-grown person, you're putting this on to a child. They cannot take it. They can't. That was one thing I learned mostly of all from him is that a person my size can actually destroy a person that size. You don't hit a child. That's the one thing I've learned from him. There's no reason in this world. If you have to hit somebody, if you have to hit a child; you better walk away. It's not worth it.

The respondent continued,

R03: The only good thing I can say about him, from him beating me all these doggone years and scars that I'll probably carry for the rest of my life, to my grave; I've never, ever hit my kids, yelled at my kids. I yell at them, I punish them. I say, "dad's mad at you and I don't like you right now." They'll go stand themselves in the corner. I don't even have to yell at these kids. Not even my stepchildren. It's great. That's the one thing that I am thankful for I never took after him when it came to beating kids. And I've always heard

stories that people who are abused usually end up being the same
way. Well, that's not right.

For most individuals, parents provide the model that is copied, as
their children become parents themselves. However, as the above
respondent indicated, for some men who had abusive childhoods, their
own experiences provide vivid and strong reactions against this
paternal behavior. The men with abusive fathers typically stated that
they wanted to parent their children differently. The following
respondent also emphasized this point. He is a 27-year-old father of
five. His mother and stepfather, whom he described as "violent",
reared him.

IER: Can you describe your parents to me?

R05: Uh. My stepfather was violent. Very violent. Um, he
used to drink a lot and then he quit, but he was still violent.
Uhh, real quick to judge. If you did something wrong, there
was no reason for it. Just that you did wrong and you
deserved to be punished, that was that. My mom on the other
hand was the protector. Mom would, you know, if we did
screw up when he wasn't home, you know, she wouldn't tell
him. Or, you know, if she did tell him she would down play
it.

This respondent indicated that the three most important things that
a father does are (1) support his children, (2) loves them, and (3) spends
quality time with them. He reported that his stepfather was a good
provider, and while this seemed to indicate that he was concerned for
his children, his abusiveness caused confusion for the respondent.

IER: Okay. And how many of those things did your dad do
with you? Or did he do for you?

R05: He supported us. You know, he always told us that he
loved us, but I uhh, when a person is violent with you, you
tend to think differently. And, as far as, you know, the quality
time with your children, we got quality time with our dad on

his two-week vacations and they only came around once a year. He worked a lot and he put a lot of long hours in and uhhh...we didn't really get a whole lot of quality time with him, but anything that we needed was there. So, and we all were aware of that, and we all knew that, because not only did we have the things that we needed, but we had the things that we wanted too. So I guess we kind of in our own way forfeited that quality time for the way that I guess he wanted to show love for us, you know. He wanted us to know that if we needed anything it was there. You don't have to worry about asking. You don't have to be afraid to ask for something, you know. You don't nag about it and don't throw a pitch and stomp your feet and whatever. But, if you need something it would be there if you wanted it, it would also be there. And so we never really got much quality time and I guess with quality time comes loving your children in a sense that if you don't spend quality time with your children, how are they to know that you love 'em.

IER: Okay. How about ...again from your perspective, thinking about your dad, what do you think were the most important things that you learned from him about being a parent?

R05: (Laughs). This is probably going to sound very odd. The things that I have learned from my dad about being a parent. The number one thing is not to be violent with my children. Take time with my children. I wanted when I was growing up so much to be able to have time with my dad. And I don't think it was because he didn't want to have time with us, I think that it was more that it became that sort of a cycle through the years while we were growing up that it wasn't something that was done intentionally or knowingly, it was more of something that was done as routine. Something that our family had just fallen into. And I'm certain that he would have like to spend more time with us and done more things with us and he just couldn't.

The next respondent is 24-year-old father of five children. He recalled for the interviewer that as a child, he had trouble "sitting still" in school and was considered a "class clown." This behavior caused him problems at home and resulted in many "whoopings" from his father. He also reported that because of these interactions, he was determined not to behave as his father.

> IER: If you think again about your dad for a minute, what do you think are the most important things that you learned from him about being a father?
>
> U28: (Long pause) Respect. Definitely respect. Punishment. What's the other word for that?
>
> IER: Discipline?
>
> U28: Yeah. Discipline, that's it. That's the big thing, that's number one, discipline. If I learned anything from him...
>
> IER: Do you discipline your kids?
>
> U28: No. That's one thing that I don't do. I don't try not to because I know how my temper is and don't want to hurt one of my children.

All of these respondents identified that they had learned "what not to do" from their abusive fathers. Still, while one may know that they do not want to behave in a particular manner, they may not know how to replace that undesired behavior. In this situation, an individual may look around his environment for examples of appropriate parental behavior. One of the respondents spoke about this.

> IER: Do you have any recollections of activities that you participated in with your parents or your family?
>
> R03: No. My mother, we used to go to church and stuff. My grandmother and grandfather used to take me everywhere. I've been to every museum. I've been to Italy. I've been to

the Bahamas. I've been all over the whole country. My grandmother would take me for two, three weeks at a time just to get me away from my dad. I mean, I would be bruised up and stuff. She was a teacher for forty some years. I loved this lady. She was like my mom. My grandfather was like my dad. I mean, if I got punished from my grandfather, there was a reason. But he taught me a lot. He taught me about everything. Not my mother and father, though. I mean, I played on little league baseball. My father never showed up. I'd go fishing, he never wanted to go. When I was in the boy scouts and stuff my mother and father never participated with that. My grandmother got involved with everything and it was just the way it was I guess. They were more my parents than my parents were.

IER: Did you get to see them pretty frequently?

R03: Every weekend. I spent from Friday to Sunday with them people. Everything they needed done, I'd go over there and move wood for them, plant the garden. They would take me down to the (thinks out loud) what would they call it in them days…the farmer shop, it was like a little restaurant. Went there every weekend with them. They tried. I mean, they knew what I was going through. My grandfather would get phone calls, I was in the hospital in the middle of the night.

The respondent had reported that his parents, and his father in particular, had taught him not to be abusive, but had taught him nothing further. The interviewer was interested in what he had learned from his mother and grandparents.

IER: What did you learn from her [your mother] about being a parent?

R03: Not very much. Really, not very much at all. She just wasn't the kind of mother I've seen other kids with when I was a kid. I always wanted other kids' parents. I had a lady friend, her name was Corky, my friend Tony was her son. We were the best of friends. When I'd run away, I'd run to her house. She wouldn't tell my parents where I was. She would hide me. She would always take care of us. She made sure I ate. She would take my sisters out for sodas. Anything they'd want. I wanted that mother. This lady loved her children. She was always there for them. It was really sad to watch those kids because they had everything I wanted. And I felt bad. We stayed friends for years and years.

IER: What did you learn from your grandparents then?

R03: Everything. My grandfather was an American Indian. He taught me about respecting nature. If you have to cut a tree down, you better use that wood for good purposes. How to build a house. I'm a carpenter by trade, that's what I do. My grandmother taught me about schooling, how to cook. Because she knew one day, I was the only son, so I would be on my own one day. "You have to learn to cook." "You have to do these things." How to do in the garden. My grandfather taught me to drive. He took my sisters all the time. Took them to museums. They taught me about all the finer things in life. Antiques that I wanted to learn about. Going to the Natural Museum of History, you know, the planetariums. They taught me about the sky, everything. There was nothing these people didn't teach me. They taught me right from wrong. You shouldn't go out drinking like you dad does. Christmas is for family. You know, we'd go there and all my cousins and everything would show up. We had "Christmas" at my grandparent's house. I'd go home, it was like I left one dream world and walked into a nightmare. So they showed me what life is really supposed to be.

IER: What did you learn about, maybe from them, about being a parent?

R03: Oh boy.

IER: Did they teach you things about how a parent would...

R03: My grandparents used to tell me that you had to provide
for each other. My grandfather used to tell me, he'd say,
"there is no reason for a man ever to hit a woman." Because
my father used to beat on my mom. He would tell me, he'd
say, "that's why I hate your father so much for what he does to
your mother and you kids." He'd say, "whatever you do
A****, respect the woman enough that if you ever get the
feeling that you have to hit someone, turn around and walk the
heck away." He said there is no reason in the world to hit a
child or to hit a woman in this world. You got to defend
yourself, but not against them. They are smaller creatures and
it's not necessary. He said that is why we do not see eye to
eye with your dad. And my grandfather taught me, teach your
children. Everything you want them to know. Things that you
don't know. Go out and learn so that you can teach it to them.
And that's what he did. He taught me everything that and I sat
for hours absorbing things. I have houses, real estate that I
rent out to people. My grandfather had over a 100 homes that
he rented out and stuff. He taught me every part of it.
Everything I want to learn. And he left me two houses when
he died. He left me his and he left me another one, to get me
started. He didn't leave me an awful lot, he left me just
enough where I could get going. You know, he didn't spoil
me. My grandmother spoiled us (chuckles) she did. They
taught us a lot though, you know.

As this respondent indicated, by interacting with his grandparents,
and observing his friend's mother, he was able to replace the negative
behavior that his parents had exhibited, with more positive behavior as
modeled by other important people in his life. Still, this is not
foolproof, as behavior that is experienced and modeled is sometimes
difficult to change.

IER: Think again of your parents, your mom and dad and all
the things that they did as parents that you just outlined. Now
think of yourself as a dad, how have you been influenced by
your mom and dad?

U28: Not really by my dad but I've been influenced a lot by my mom. Since I've been a parent my dad has been passed, so. Basically like if I have parenting problems, I'll talk to my mom about them. If my son is acting up in school, I'll call my mom and say, "mom, the teacher said that [son] was doing such and such, cutting up in school and this and that." She would always say to me, "well, sit him down and talk to him." I mean he's only four so I can't (gestures something) "what's wrong with you dude." I can't do him like that. I wouldn't do that to him, no. I wouldn't feel right. A lot of my problems that I talk to my mom about is like when one of the kids cuts up and [I] get ready to grab them sometimes I just blank out from how my dad used to do me. We would get into words and I would just be getting my behind whooped and that was like traumatic. So that's why I try not to get upset with them. Because I know that I would whoop them and I don't want to. So I talk to my mom about it.

IER: Sometimes it's hard not fall right into those patterns. Isn't it?

U28: Yeah. Sometimes it's very hard. I'm glad that my girlfriends there. She can take care of it and I'll just go into another room and sit down. Or go outside and smoke a cigarette and sit down and go "swooh, I almost did it." I would feel...like I whooped my son once. I smacked him on the butt a couple of times. After I did it I cried because I felt bad. Because I thought about how my dad used to whoop me. I felt bad whoopin his butt. I brought him back in and told him that I was sorry. I shouldn't have whooped his butt. I should have talked to him about it. That was a couple years ago. I just can't whoop them. Their mom has to grab them up. I just can't do it.

IER: I think as adults you can actually hurt the kids. They are a lot smaller.

U28: Especially if ...I know how my temper is. If I get enraged, I would really hurt them. So I try to refrain from it. I may grab his arm at the most. Other than that, when he does something that makes me mad...like I've been trying to change that in here. Like what am I going to do when I get back out. I'm trying to change myself for when he does do something that I don't like. I can't be like, "oh, I'm not going to do nothing about it." I might have to take him right there and sit him down and wait until I calm down and do it right there so that he can see my anger and understand that I'm not mad for just no reason. I'm mad because he did something that he wasn't supposed to do. Not get all chipper and happy again. "Okay [names son], let's go sit down and talk now." I have to do it right then and there. I have to make a lot of adjustments in my parenting when I get home.

Finally, three respondents indicated that one of the most salient characteristics of their fathers' behavior was his addiction. For the most part, these fathers were addicted to alcohol, yet they were present in their children's lives. They were referred to as "functional alcoholics." The first respondent addressed this.

IER: Can you describe your parents to me?

U79: My dad was drinker, actually an alcoholic. My mother was left to do all the disciplining and all that. I guess he was a functional alcoholic. He worked. He had a couple jobs. He was a boilermaker and he drove a cab on the side. They were loving parents. My dad wasn't abusive. He was an alcoholic. Like he worked during the day and pretty much get drunk at night. I never remember him drinking during the day. He was always drunk at night. Never abusive. I never even seen him hit one of the my brothers or sisters. My mother always did the discipline. They were pretty good parents. They made sure we got what we needed.

IER: If you had to choose five words to describe your dad?

U79: Loving, caring, compassionate, faithful. I remember he was always faithful to my mother. She always told us that. Honest. He didn't lie about nothing.

Another respondent also recalled that while his father drank, he was present and supportive of his children.

IER: Could you describe your parents to me?

U33: My father, as of now he is 81 now, he worked a lot, most of his life. He drank but he was not a violent drunk. For the most part he took care of his family pretty much, pretty well, too. We never wanted for anything. We never starved for anything.

IER: If you had to pick five words to describe him?

U33: That's very interesting (chuckles). I would give him, kind, gentle, caring, loving and basically just dad.

IER: What kinds of activities did you participate in with your parents?

U33: Hmm. Well, growing up just basically, we would go out to dinner sometimes, just me and my parents. My father used to take me to work sometimes on the weekends. He did construction. He was a foreman and he would take me on the job sites to work with him. He would have me spray different things around. He would pay me to do this for the weekend. I participated in that with him. Other than that there was not many other activities that we did together.

The final respondent had a much different recollection of his stepfather. He was reared by his mother and stepfather and recounted that both were alcoholics. He reported that his parents seemed more concerned about drinking than they did about taking care of their children. This respondent did not consider his stepfather as his "dad."

IER: Did you consider your stepfather to be your "dad?"

U95: No, he was abusive toward my mom. He hurt her a couple of times, physically, she was in a neck-brace, in the hospital a couple of times. He was a drunk. He was a guard at the [name of] penitentiary for quite a few years. He was in the military, he was in Vietnam, and then he came back and was at the "wall" and then after he quit there he had a couple of floating jobs. From the time he worked down there he was nothing but an alcoholic. To this day he still drinks. I'm surprised he isn't dead the way he drinks. He still works, though; the alcohol hasn't kept him from working.

IER: How close are you to your stepfather?

U95: I'm not...he was no role model. Of course if I wanted to be a drunk that would be the way to go. There was no incentive, you know, "maybe you should do this in your life," or "stay in school," or any direction. There was really no concern about ...I think the only concern I ever seen was that there was food on the table and there were clothes on our backs.

Two of the respondents with "addicted" fathers indicated that their alcoholism did not prevent them from playing an active role in their children's lives, from the respondents' perspectives. The third indicated that his stepfather's alcoholism did impact his ability to effectively parent.

As outlined above, the respondents reported a wide array of paternal behavior. Unfortunately, most of the incarcerated fathers experienced unpleasant relationships with their own fathers.

Paternal and Maternal Roles

The men who participated in the interviews were asked to describe the three most important things that a father does and a mother does for their children. Table 9 highlights their responses. Interestingly, the interview respondents stated that the two most important things that a parent (mother and father) does for his or her children is to support them and show love for them.

According to the respondents, a father should (1) financially support, (2) love, and (3) set an example for his children. From their perspective, a mother should (1) provide emotional support, (2) love, and (3) set an example for her children.

Table 9: Most Important Things Parents Do For Their Children

Father	Respondents	Mother	Respondents
Financial	16	Emotional	12
Loves Them	11	Loves Them	11
Teaches	11	Teaches	8
Spends Time	8	Spends Time	6
Emotional	5	Takes Care Of	4
Protects	2	Protects	2
Disciplines	2	Disciplines	3
Communicates	1	Communicates	2
Keeps Promises	1	Financial Support	1

The respondents also noted that both parents should spend quality time with their children. It seems as though the respondents have identified that parents should be supportive, loving and present in their child's life. Interestingly, only three respondents identified discipline as one of the three most important things that a father or mother does.

The respondents were further asked to "rate" the performance of their parents, giving them a composite score from 1-10 on the qualities and characteristics that they had identified. Table 10 provides the composite scores that the interviewees gave their parents. Not surprisingly, the men with "Absent" fathers rated their fathers' performance lower than any other paternal type, while they rated their mothers' performance higher than any other respondent group. Also of interest, is that the men with "Abusive" fathers rated both mother and father lowest on parenting. Not surprisingly, the group that had the highest ratings of their fathers' performance was the men who had "Loving and Supportive" fathers.

Table 10: Composite Scores of Parents by Paternal Model

Model	Father's Score (1-10)	Mother's Score (1-10)
Absent (n = 10)	3.88	9.4
Abusive (n = 3)	5.33	6.67
Addict (n = 3)	6.33	6.33
Workaholic (n = 4)	8.87	8.87
Loving and Supportive (n = 5)	9.0	7.9

SUMMARY

The respondents in the current study were relatively young Black and White fathers who were jailed for non-violent offenses. They are high school educated with low rates and levels of employment.

The incarcerated fathers in the present study were primarily reared in two-parent families, although their experiences ranged from the very positive to the very negative. Twenty-percent of the interview respondents (n = 5) reported that a parent had been incarcerated and in the majority of cases, it was the father. Forty percent of the interview respondents grew to adulthood with no father figure present in their lives, and four interview respondents (16%) experienced horrible abuse at the hands of their fathers.

Attachment theory posits that all children have a wide array of "pathways" (Bowlby, 1988) along which to develop. The developmental pathway that an individual takes is "determined by the environment he meets with, especially the way his parents (or parent substitutes) treat him, and how he responds to them" (Bowlby, 1988, p. 136). The experiences that we have in childhood, and the kind of parenting to which we are exposed, has an influence in our later lives. The following chapter will explicate the ways in which the respondents' childhood experiences impact their paternal behavior.

CHAPTER 4
Jailed Fathers in their Current Family
The Seed Grows

"It is the moment where hopes and fears converge, where yesterday and forever collide. It is the moment that shapes everything that comes after, the moment you become somebody's father"
Leonard Pitts, Jr. (1999)

Many of the jailed fathers in the present study had adverse experiences in their childhood, including fractured families, parental incarceration, and paternal models that were abusive or non-existent. The impact of these difficult experiences is carried to adulthood and parenthood. Unfortunately, as described below, many of the jailed fathers were unprepared for the moment they became somebody's father.

PARENTAL STATUS OF THE STUDY SAMPLE

Table 11 provides an overview of the parental status of the respondents. These were deduced from the respondents' reports regarding the number of minor children they had and the number that they resided with prior to incarceration (see items 14 – 17). Ninety-two respondents reported on their parental status. Five of the 92 respondents (5.4%) had adult children only, and four respondents (4.3%) reported that their child had been born during their incarceration. Hence, 83 respondents had minor children prior to their arrest and incarceration. Thirty-seven of the 83 respondents (44.6%) were residing with some or all of their minor children prior to their incarceration. The remaining 46 respondents (55.4%) resided with none of their minor children prior to their incarceration (see Table 11).

Table 11: Parental Status of Respondents

Parental Status	Number	Percentage
All Children over 18	n = 5	5.4%
Child was born during father's incarceration	n = 4	4.3%
"Parents" – Lived with all minor children	n = 17	18.5%
"Mixed Parents" – Lived with some, but not all, minor children	n = 20	21.8%
"Biological Fathers" – Lived with no minor children	n = 46	50%
Totals	N = 92	100%

Characteristics of the Current Family

The respondents in the study were asked a series of questions regarding their current family structure. One of the issues that became clear during the pilot study (Hanrahan et al, 1996; Martin et al, 1995) was that imprisoned fathers typically had very complex family structures and living arrangements prior to incarceration. It was anticipated that the jailed fathers in the current study would have similarly complex family structures. Rather than force the men to categorize their prior living arrangements (as in the pilot study), the fathers were asked, "in the six months prior to your incarceration, whom did you live with for the most part?" The fathers were asked to check every option that applied. The fathers were further asked to indicate the number of minor children with whom they had resided prior to incarceration[4]. Table 12 presents questionnaire information on the jailed fathers' living arrangements.

Twenty respondents reported two or more living arrangements in the six months prior to incarceration, which is indicative of some tumult in the personal lives of the respondents. Thirty-seven of the jailed fathers (39.8%) reported living with minor children in the six months prior to incarceration. While 15 men reported living with their "Wife only" or "Wife and children," nearly one-half of the respondents reported living with their "Girlfriend" (27%) or their "Girlfriend and children" (23%). Hence, while nearly 66% of the jailed fathers were in a living arrangement with a woman, only 16% were married

---

[4] There were validity problems with these questions because some men who had indicated in the first question that they lived with their "Girlfriend only" or "Wife only" also reported living with children in a later question. It appears that the men may have checked the first response that applied in the first question (rather than all that applied) and moved on to the next question. During coding, it was decided that if the fathers reported living with minor children in the latter question, it would also be coded as such in the first.

Table 12: Living Arrangements for 6 Months Prior to Jail Term

Lived with Girlfriend and Children	n = 21 (22.6%)
Lived with Girlfriend, No Children	n = 25 (26.9%)
Lived with Wife and Children	n = 12 (12.9%)
Lived with Wife, No Children	n = 3 (3.2%)
Lived alone with Children	n = 3 (3.2%)
Lived Alone	n = 18 (19.4%)
Lived with Parents	n = 17 (18.3%)
Lived with Parents and Children	n = 1 (1.07%)
Lived with Friends	n = 7 (7.5%)
Lived with other relatives	n = 5 (5.4%)
Other	n = 2 (2.2%)

Percentage totals do not equal 100 because men could check multiple categories

Number of Children

The fathers in the study had a total of 248 children, 115 sons and 133 daughters. Most of these (n = 186, 75%) were minor children. The fathers had 103 minor daughters, with an average age of 7.32 years, and 83 minor sons, with an average age of 8.25 years. Therefore, the jailed fathers had an average of 2.0 minor children with an average age of 7.7 years. In this respect, the respondents in the present study were strikingly similar to the 402,434 state prisoners surveyed in 1991 that had an average of 2.05 minor children (Beck, et al, 1993).

As mentioned above, 37 of the jailed fathers who had minor children were residing with at least some of these children prior to their incarceration. The vast majority (87%) of these children were now residing with their mother.

Fathers' Beliefs Regarding and Participation in Childrearing

The fathers were asked a series of questions regarding their beliefs about the parent who is the most important with regard to certain childrearing activities, such as scheduling appointments, providing discipline, making decisions, and providing financial support. The fathers were also asked who was the more important parent in terms of their children's overall development. With the exception of scheduling appointments, the majority of the respondents indicated that both parents are equally important in childrearing. There was only one area (financial support) where fathers were rated as more important than mothers, and not by much. The results are highlighted below.

Table 13: Fathers' Perceptions Regarding Childrearing

Who is more important for?	Mother	Father	Both are Equally Important
Scheduling appointments	58.2%	2.2%	39.6%
Financial Support	15.4%	18.7%	65.9%
Discipline	19.8%	17.6%	62.6%
Making Decisions	22.8%	7.6%	69.6%
Child's Overall Development	21.4%	4.4%	74.4%

It is evident that the reports of the fathers indicate their beliefs that both mothers and fathers play critical roles in the lives of their children. However, beliefs and behavior do not always correspond. An effort was made to gauge how frequently the respondents participated in childrearing activities such as spending time with their children, disciplining them or interacting with them about a school activity.

The frequency of interactions ranged from "not at all" to "daily." These items were combined to form the "Parental Behavioral Index for Resident Children", which has a range of 0-16. It could be expected that the respondents who lived with some or all of their children would have interacted with these children on a regular basis. This expectation was confirmed. Nearly 90% of the "parents" and "mixed fathers" reported weekly or daily interactions with their resident children (see Figure 1)

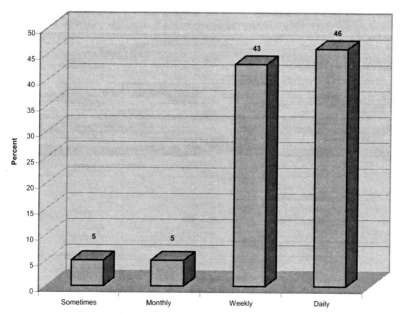

Figure 1: Parents and Mixed fathers' (n = 37) interactions with resident children

It was also anticipated that the respondents who resided apart from some or all of their minor children ("biological" and "mixed" fathers) would have less frequent interactions with these non-resident children. Still, the lack of interaction is surprising as 70% of the respondents reported interacting with their non-resident children monthly or less than monthly (See Figure 2).

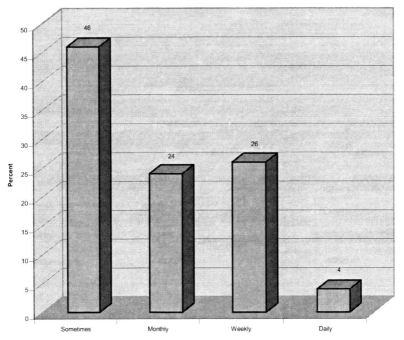

Figure 2: Biological and Mixed Fathers' (n = 66) interactions with non-resident children

Paternal Behavior

Attachment theory suggests that men parent in a way similar to that which they experienced as children (Bowlby, 1988). Further, attachment theory suggests that both the mother and father are attachment figures for their children and that there are qualitative differences in the way each fulfills their role. "In most families with young children the father's role is a different one. He is more likely to engage in physically active and novel play than the mother and, especially for boys, to become his child's preferred play companion" (Bowlby, 1988, p. 11).

The interview respondents provided support for the tenets of attachment theory. The important point that needs to be emphasized is that the respondents who were living with their children (n = 13) were involved in the lives of their children, especially the ones with whom they resided in the cases of the mixed parents. They were able to describe subtle differences in their personalities, and they were able to provide detailed accounts of the kinds of interactions that they had with their children. It became evident from these fathers that their paternal role was an important one, and one they took seriously.

The following respondent is a "mixed parent" of four children. The interviewer asked him about his role as a father and his relationship with his children.

> IER: On a scale of one to ten with one being not important and ten being extremely important, how important is your role as a father?

> U01: I think it is a ten. Really important.

> IER: Are there any roles that are more important?

> U01: No. I think being a father is a ten because it's control you have over someone else's life. You're molding this person. The things that you do or say or act or the way you are around them is going to define the type of person that they are going to grow up to be. So I think that's really important. Being a husband is important but I wouldn't put it up to a ten

because you have your own personality and you're just combining two personalities...two set personalities. Being a father is like you are in control of that personality. You are going to shape and mold that personality. What they are going to become. What they are going to be. You're not going to make them a rocket scientist or a star athlete or anything like that but as far as an everyday individual you have the greatest input. It's the type of citizen that they are going to turn out to be. So I think that's why it would be a ten.

IER: Tell me what being a father means to you.

U01: It means everything. It means the world. I rank that up there with one of the most important things of my life. It's pretty important.

IER: Can you describe to me your relationship with your kids prior to your incarceration? Did they have any activities that they did with you or special kinds of activities?

U01: Recently because [son] is older, he's ten now, but he started to play basketball. We were given chances to play basketball together. I was teaching him the fundamental drills. My daughters, we used to wrestle and roughhouse and play around. My thing is that I hate to be tickled so they used to jump on me and tickle me. So that was several of the things that we used to do around the house. Things like that. My son, [we played] Play Station and that. We got to do that. He was able to play that and we got time to do that. I used to take them out to the movies all the time. It would be a day that they got to choose what to do. What they wanted to do. One time I sat through three movies. Goofy movies. Godzilla, Toy Soldiers, goofy things that they wanted to do. Sometimes I would just let them be kids. I would spoil them because I was rough on them as far as school. So I try to even that out and make a balance. Sometimes I would just spoil them a lot. We did a lot of things together. Mostly they were younger and there was a lot of stuff like movies and things like that but it was starting to get more to basketball with [son]. [Daughter] because she's tall for her age, she was starting to play basketball too. [Younger daughter], we never got to do things together. [With her] being younger and being a girl, we didn't get to do a lot. I used to pull her on her roller blades or something. That was about it. Other than that it was just more like movies or things like that.

In many instances the activities between a father and his children revolved around "playing," yet this seemed dependent upon the personality of the father and the ages, gender, and personality of the children, as indicated by the next respondent. He is a parent of five young children. The interviewer asked him about his role as a father and his relationship with his children.

IER: Okay. You told me this a while ago that the three most important things that a father does are support his kids, spend quality time with them and love them? Do you do those things for your kids?

R05: Yes. Yes I do.

IER: And what do you think is your most important role or job as a father?

R05: I would have to say spend quality time with my children would be the most important. I believe, that uh…you are what you learn. And, as a child if you learn not to be home, if you learn to do nothing but work, you know, if you learn not to spend quality time with your family then you are not going to do it. I started out that way. And I made a change. I didn't want to be my dad. I wanted to support my family and I wanted to love my kids but I wanted also to spend quality time with them. I wanted my kids to know that they were loved. I wanted my kids to know that if they needed someone to talk to they could trust dad. I wanted them to know that if they wanted…they needed information about something they could trust dad. And I want, I have my own little thing with each child too. You know, umm, with my oldest son, I shoot bow a lot. Uhhmm, and I go to archery shoots, bow and arrow, you know. And he showed some interest in it. So I bought him a little toy bow and he liked it and he shot all the time. He'd shoot. So one day whenever we were at the bow shop and I had a couple hundred extra dollars on me I asked him if he wanted a new bow. And I bought him a good bow, I bought him what was actually a woman's bow. And I just put a longer string on it and turned it down and worked on it and made it to where he could pull it back. And he just loves that thing to death. He's seven years old. He's got four first place trophies, you know, for archery. And I'm so proud of him. That boy he just…instead of running around the neighborhood or bugging his mother or making a mess or fighting with his brothers or sisters, he would rather take his bow outside and shoot at a target. And that boy will go out there and he will shoot for hours, hours. He comes home from school sometimes he'll shoot till dark. And I think that is a good quality. I think that something...because...I taught him how to shoot. I taught him how to handle the bow. I taught him what is proper to shoot at and what is not proper to shoot at. He's very safe. I still supervise him, when he shoots, but I know that I don't have to coach him anymore. I know that he knows what he's doin. And it gives me a good feeling to know, hey, I took this little baby and you know now he's knee high to a grasshopper and I taught him what to do. I taught him. He has fun. He loves it. And my daughter, I'll play Barbie dolls with her. That's not beyond me. That's my daughter. I don't care what anybody says, you know. So we play, umm. sometimes we'll set and have tea. I don't play, you know…we'll make real tea. You know, we'll set and have real tea. My son, you know, it's not beyond him to turn a wrench either. I'm working on a car putting a transmission in, you know, my son can tell you every part of a car. He can tell you what a drive shaft is, he can tell you what a transmission is, an engine, an intake, a carburetor, you know. My [younger] son, he likes to play baseball. I hate baseball. I don't know why. Sports. I'm not a sports oriented person. Other than hunting, I'm not

sports oriented. And, well, [son] likes it. So we play baseball.
I throw the ball, he hits it, you know. And, I 'll go runnin after
it and he'll try and tackle me and you know I think he gets his
sports mixed up. I touch the ball and he tries to tackle me. I'll
fall over and just it's more or less nothin special, just kind of a
bond between he and I. But, I spend time with him and the
same with the twins. But they're so young yet that I can't
identify what is really important to them…what they really
like to do. So I just do what I can to spend time with them.

As this respondent indicated, fathers who are involved parents will
recognize that each child has a unique personality and interests. Thus,
he participated in the activities that were important to them, rather than
force his interests on them. Some of the fathers spoke not only of
"playing" with their children, but of other kinds of activities, as well.

One of the dilemmas facing the "mixed parents" is that they are
living with some of their children, but not all of them. As highlighted
above, in Figures 1 and 2, the amount of contact is much greater
between fathers and their resident children. The "mixed parents" are
aware of this time differential among their children. The following
respondent discusses his regret and sadness at not being able to spend
more time with his biological sons, who reside with their mother in
another state. This respondent indicated that he tried to make up for the
lack of contact with his biological sons by spending time with his
fiancée's children.

IER: You told me earlier that the three most important things
that a father does are, not in this order: love his children,
physically supports them and is there for them. I think you
were maybe talking about "there" to do activities with them
and those things. Did you do these things for your children?

U33: Yes. Basically as far as [his sons], the only thing I was
there for them for was financially, to support them. Because
they live in another city and I don't see them that often. When
they do come to town or if I go there, we go do things. We
play sports together and stuff like that. I don't think that's
sufficient enough. I'm not satisfied with that. It sort of hurts

me that I can't be there to do more with them everyday on a regular basis; or even if it was weekly or monthly regular basis. But I would like it to be something and it's not.

IER: How often do you see them, would you estimate?

U33: Geez. The last time I saw them was three years ago, Fathers' Day. I try to send them...I send them gifts. If I call and it's around report card time or whatever, I'll send them money for getting good grades. That's not enough. I can never do enough for them because I'm not there to support them. Financially, you can send money around the world but if you're not there physically for your children to do things with them, to support them in what their interests are then all the money in the world means nothing. It really does. It means nothing. My father, we didn't do a lot of sports together because he was older then but he supported me in the things that I did. I played baseball. I played football and he didn't come to the games or nothing but he was supportive in that he knew that I could do it. He showed his support in a different way which was helpful to me. I didn't get angry with him that he couldn't come to the games or anything like that. But I think the father has to be there physically, you know. My two boys, that's impossible. But I get my satisfaction with [fiancées son]. He and I, we do everything. He's a good kid. He's intelligent. He loves to read. He loves math. When he comes home from school, we go in the house and he has a little personal computer. He gets his computer out and he's so like ready to go all the time. When it comes to learning, that impresses me because I think, well, his biological father is really missing out. Like I missed out for my boys and I wish I could be there. I could have been there for them. I get a lot of satisfaction out of this. A lot of satisfaction. It's like, it feels so good to come home and sit there and show him how to do his homework or I'll give him a chance to do it first and then we'll review it together. Then I'll point out his mistakes and erase the mistakes and I'll give him another chance to correct them. He's like real gung-ho about doing homework. He loves homework. He doesn't like to miss school. My relationship with him has grown tremendously over the last, I'd say, the last two to three years. I spend more time with my fiancée's children than she does. For me, I'm very satisfied. I feel bad being away from them now. For some mistakes that I made that were not wise choices. So...but I've learned here. This time is the last time because I don't have four or five months to give away. Because of my children. I miss my children more than I miss my fiancée. Well, her children more than I miss her.

IER: On a scale, then, from one to ten, how important to you is your role as a father?

U33: I'd say ten. Again, because my important role as a father, this is meaning with [fiancée's children], it's very important right now for them for me to be their father because their father has lied to them tremendously. He does nothing for them, doesn't support them. He's promised them everything and given them nothing. I feel that he has robbed them. I don't have a lot of anger towards him but I don't approve of what he's done to his children. I don't support anything that he has to say or do with his children. Because he's told them, "oh yeah, I'll come and take you Christmas shopping. I'll do this for you, I'll do that for you." Then he turns around and they're waiting for him, you know, bags packed or whatever waiting at the door looking for him. And I always tell them, "he's not coming." I know he did drugs in the past or is doing drugs now but to set a child up like that and to keep hurting them like that is wrong. I think that is so wrong. I even feel guilty when I'm not there to take them to the park. Let alone, blow them off every single time. He's called on their birthday one time in the last four years. Told them he was coming to pick them up and bringing their birthday gift over and he never made it. Never even returned phone call or nothing. It's very important as my role as a father for those two children. It's very important because they have nobody else.

It has been the author's observation that there is a prevailing belief that incarcerated men are not good fathers. It is true that when a father is arrested and jailed that his children suffer from his mistakes. However, many parents make mistakes that cause suffering among their children, and making mistakes is not sufficient to label individuals as "bad parents." As the respondents indicated above, the paternal role is an integral one for the "parents" and "mixed parents." These fathers' accounts of interactions with their children show warmth and caring. They spent time with their children and were supportive of them. These respondents were "good" fathers who made "bad" decisions.

There were other men, however, who were, by their own accounts, "bad" fathers who made "bad" decisions. These respondents were the "biological fathers," men who resided with none of their children prior to incarceration and had infrequent contact. One of the interesting themes that emerged from the interviews with the "biological fathers" was the disjuncture between (1) the respondents' beliefs about the behavior of a "good" father and the significance of the father role, and (2) their actions in fulfilling this role. All of the men clearly articulated what it meant to be a father, and this typically included: (1) taking care of their children's financial needs, (2) spending quality time with their children, (3) teaching or guiding children and providing a good example, (4) being emotionally supportive, and (5) showing love for their children. Unfortunately, by their own accounts, these men were not living up to their own standard of a "good father."

The first respondent is a 35-year-old father of four children by four different women. By his account he had "loving and supportive" parents who reared him well.

IER: You briefly described your parents already. If you had to choose five words to describe your dad, what words would you use?

U93: Great, extraordinary, loving, understanding and whole lot of stability.

IER: Sounds like you have very warm memories of your dad.

U93: Just like well up.

IER: What about your mom? What five words would you use to describe her?

U93: Home-made, down-to-earth, much love, determined and a lot of stability.

IER: In your opinion, what are the three most important things that a father does for his children?

U93: Nurture, guide and provide.

IER: Did you dad do those things?

U93: Ah yeah! I just can't get it. I don't know what it is. I probably had one of the best teachers you could show a child the love that a father's supposed to....I don't know what it is. I don't know what it is. I don't know why I can't get it.

The interviewer asked the respondent if he had done these three things for his children and he reported that he had not. The interviewer was interested in the respondent's perception of the importance of the paternal role.

IER: How important is being a father to you?

U93: It's very important. It's like any other animal. You take...like any other animal. It's important that the father be there. Because you want your kid to make the best decisions. What way to make a better decision for yourself then you got it from your father and he's living right too. When you know that your parents are living right more likely you know, this is it. They ain't looking for no guidance that strong outside of the family because they can get it right at home.

IER: If you had again to put it on a scale of one to ten, how important is being a father?

U93: Ah it's a ten. Definitely.

IER: Are you living up to your own expectations?

U93: No. Those are some big shoes to fill. I'm just trying to get it. Some people holler at me but it's hard. Especially with all the negative outside influences that you have. Parent's got to go up against so much. I ain't never been no parent. I ain't got no parenting skills I don't think. I asked a couple guys about how can I gain my children's trust and interest in me. A guy told me that you got to be manipulative. You got to manipulate their mind. I said, "What?" He said, "yeah man. You got to give them something to draw them a little closer to you." I don't know if that's called parenting skills or what. I don't know. I don't want to get so desperate that I be willing to try anything. Then it looks real ugly.

IER: Tell me what being a father means to you. Tell me what is a father?

U93: What is a father? A father is somebody that is there constantly. A father is someone who plays a part in a younger person's life. A sibling. A father who takes care of the home, his wife. A father is the person who sets the house on it's course in terms of the morals that he got.

IER: It seems like you learned a lot of that from your father.

U93: From his actions. But I just can't live it. I don't know why.

IER: Do you have any insight into that?

U93: But you know what. When I had my first child, that was [son's name]. My expectations and my self-esteem was so high. I was thinking military and marriage. Then that relationship went to the challenge. Because my mother told me that "you wouldn't know what love was if it snuck up behind you and bit you." So I claimed to know what I was getting into. But they kept telling me, "that ain't it." You giving me some half information. I kept saying, "what ain't it." Instead of just saying, "that girl ain't for you." She's didn't, but she allowed me to get burnt. So I can't see myself right. I don't know. I guess from that bad experience because I would say, "I want to have all my children by that one woman." But every time I met a woman and I went off to an institution, she didn't stick around. Four times that happened.

As the respondent reported, he had high expectations of entering into a committed relationship with one woman, much like his own parents had. However, this dream unraveled when he was first incarcerated and he seemed surprised that his girlfriend(s) did not stay committed to him through his incarceration. By his account, he has been incarcerated for 10 of the last 13 years.

The following respondent is a 23-year-old father of three daughters by three different women. He has two four-year-old daughters and a four-month old daughter. The respondent told the interviewer that his paternal role was one of the most important roles he fulfills.

IER: Tell me what being a father means to you.

U29: To me it means making sure that your kids be brought up in the right direction. Going in the right direction. Making sure that they do everything to the best of their ability. Like we were talking about making sure that they are well taken care of. To the best of your ability. Making sure that they see you doing the things that you would like for them to be doing. Not doing anything out of the ordinary that you wouldn't like for them to pick up off you. Caring for them. Putting them first. Kids should be your first priority. They didn't ask to come here. You brought them here. They should be your first priority in life.

IER: Were they your first priority?

U29: Yes. They were.

The respondent told the interviewer that the three most important things that a father does are (1) spend time with his children, (2) take care of them, and (3) make sure they know he loves them. The interviewer asked the respondent if he did those things.

U29: I took care of them very well. I always told them that I loved them. I can say that too. But it's just the time thing. I was always running. I'd come home and bring them something home and think that was good. Little time I spent at home, I felt that was all good. Sit and watch TV with them. Fix them a bowl of cereal in the morning, that type of thing. I was around but I never did nothing with them. You are supposed to take kids to the park, take them to the zoo or Discovery Zone or something. I wasn't doing that type of stuff. I take them outside in the yard for a minute. Let them play around while I'm out there. I wasn't doing the time thing that I should have been.

IER: If I were able to ask your daughters to rate you, what do you think they would give you?

U29: Probably give me ... they'd probably give me about a seven. [names daughter], the youngest one, she had have to give me a ten. Because I was there all the time with her. But the other ones, they would have to give me a seven. Considering that I didn't live with neither one of them, but they'd have to give me about a seven. Because I did take care of them. I did tell them that I loved them all the time. And don't get me wrong, I did spend time with them but I didn't spend enough. At least I don't feel that spent enough. Maybe I was. I wasn't just always, always running. I'd be at the house. I don't know. I'm just saying that I wasn't doing enough with them.

The above respondent recognized that he was falling short of his own standard of being a "good" father, yet he seemed to want to believe that his children would rate his performance as "above average." While this seems unlikely, many of the "biological father" respondents seemed to suggest that they were doing the best that they could, and their children would recognize this.

The next respondent is a 30-year-old father of three children. He described growing up without a father. The interviewer later asked him if his parents had influenced him.

> IER: Now, if you think one more time about your parents and all the things that they did as parents or things that they didn't do as parents and now think about yourself as a father. Do you think that you've been influenced by your parents?
>
> U81: More or less my dad. He was never around. I'm not around for my kids.
>
> IER: So you think that you learned that from your dad?
>
> U81: I think that I don't pay any attention to my kids because my dad didn't pay any attention to me. It's not that I learned it from him, it's just basically I grew up without a father and my mother she remarried but I was moving out when she remarried.

The respondent was not living with any of his children at the time of his arrest. The respondent stated that the most important things a father does are (1) making sure that children's financial needs are met, and (2) "keeping them in line."

> IER: Did you do those things for your children?
>
> U81: I always took them a little present or something like that on the holidays. [Names son], I get to spend time with him and talk to him. He was only two years old then. It's been a while since I've seen any of my kids.
>
> IER: Can you describe what being a father means to you?

U81: He has to be responsible and he really should be there helping to raise the kids regardless if he's with the mother or not. He should still play a part in raising them. Spend time with the kids. If you don't spend time with the kids, the kids have trouble identifying themselves because they're around different people and stuff. I think growing up.

IER: Did you do those things?

U81: Spend a lot of time with them? No.

IER: How close did you feel to your kids before you were incarcerated?

U81: I wasn't close to them at all.

IER: So you really didn't have a strong relationship with them.

U81: No.

As this respondent stated, the father-child relationship should be independent of the adult, "husband-wife" relationship. Unfortunately, the relationship between father and child seemed completely dependent upon the relationships between these men and the mothers of their children. As the following respondent indicates, the adult relationships are often very fragile and are borne from a sexual relationship. This respondent was young when he became a father, and he did not put a lot of thought or planning into parenthood.

IER: Tell me about your daughter. Do you have one daughter?

U92: My daughter. That's my girl.

IER: How old is she?

U92: She's ten. I take her out all the time. She always calls me, "dad I'm ready. C'mon and get me." I'll take her to

Chunky Cheese or go-cart riding or laser tag shoot-out. My little nephew is about her age and they play all the time. Those two are inseparable. She looks just like me but with long hair. She's always energetic and always wanting…Sometimes I might not have time and she'll be mad. Like, "why aren't you coming to get me?" Then she'll go with my sister. Her aunt and spend time with her. I try my best to be there for her.

IER: You were pretty young when you had her.

U92: Yeah. It was the first time. I didn't know nothing about it and two seconds and ten months later I found out I had the kid.

IER: So you were about 18?

U92: No I was 17/18.

IER: So she wasn't a planned pregnancy.

U92: Never planned. It was just something spontaneous happened and didn't know what I was doing. Was never able to enjoy nothing. Just two seconds and went home and didn't think nothing about it. That's about it.

Again, this respondent described the significance of a father in his child's life, yet he was not living up to his own standard.

IER: On a scale of one to ten, with one being not important and ten being very important, how to important to you is your role as a father?

U92: Me as a father for my daughter it's about a seven. I haven't been around lately but I'm important to her.

IER: Tell me what a father means to you. What is a father?

U92: A father is hard to explain. It's a whole lot. A father is everything. Should be. A father is what ever is there. Whatever comes to him he should be able…a father in my definition should be a catcher's mitt. Whatever is thrown at him he should be able to catch and be able to throw back at the kid. Should be there. Support them. The pitcher is the kid. The pitcher is always throwing something and the father should be the catcher's mitt where he is always able to catch it. Help…throw back at it…throw it again…throw back, throw again…He's always going to be there and you've have to you go to the pitcher's mound and say, "look here, this is what I want you to do. This is how you should do. Because I've been here and I know this batter. I know what he is about so throw a curve ball so he can't hit, so you. That's what my definition is.

IER: In your opinion, the amount of time that you spend with [daughter], which is about every weekend, is that enough time to be there. To be the catcher as you are describing it.

U92: No. Not really. It's just barely enough. By me, my lifestyle that I was living, running around in the streets doing this, trying to make, whatever; every time she needs I'm always here giving. Just buying her what ever she wanted. I got her everything that she wanted. She was happy but my lifestyle…I could sit down on the weekend and settle down. During the week day I'm here and here taking care of this, taking care of that which I have try to get some work.

IER: You mentioned that your dad as you were growing up often was not around. He gave you material things but…

U92: And that's what…I was going the wrong way. Sometimes it is meant for people to be incarcerated and I was just walking the same footsteps as him but I keep thinking the weekend would solve everything. She was happy. She was always looking forward to it. I don't know if I could sit there and really take custody of her because I wasn't having no legal job or things like that. I would love to. I at least have the weekend. My dad never did that on the weekends either. On the weekends he'd want to lay back and watch the sports and golf and car racing and drink his beer. He never wanted to do things. Me, I can't do that. The weekdays I see her and say, "here, you need something. You want to go shopping?" But on the weekends we do activities. I'll take her fishing, barbequing and things like that.

The next respondent is a 34-year-old father of three children by the same mother. He was in the ninth grade when his girlfriend became pregnant for the first time and the respondent seemed to indicate little control over this event.

IER: Can you describe for me a typical day when you were growing up?

U03: Typical day as far as what do you mean? When I was in school?

IER: You can decide. When you were in school, summer vacation...

U03: That's kind of hard. When I was in school, when I was in high school I was living with my brother. Ninth grade I come to have a son. That's my first son. It was alright. My brother was good to me. The only mistake that I thought was a mistake at the time was when I impregnated my kid's mother at that time because I was so young. My days back then were like any other typical teenager beside that little set back there. I played sports. I graduated from high school and everything.

This respondent spoke of being reared by his older brother and his sister-in-law, and he spoke warmly of them both. His father was "Absent" after the respondent's mother died when the respondent was a year old. The respondent indicated repeatedly that a father has to physically "be there" for his children.

IER: What did you learn from your brother about being a parent?

U03: What did I learn from him? Be there for them no matter what too. Every activity. Spend time with them. I'd be there to correct them when they are wrong. Congratulate them when they're right. Things like that.

IER: You have to be there.

U03: Yeah. You have to be there.

IER: Okay. You told me earlier that the three most important things that a father does: love his children, teach them – have them set goals for themselves and kind of show them how to do that, but also be an example for them. Did you do those things for your children?

U03: The first two I can say I'm pretty much… I love my children with all my heart. Without a doubt. You can't stop that. Nothing will come between that. As far as setting goals, me myself, I don't think so. I don't think…I've set the wrong example, put it that way. By me coming to jail. This is not the first time. This is like the third time. The charges aren't nothing bad. It's just the fact that I'm in jail and they don't like that. When they come down here to see me, I can see it. They are pissed at me because I shouldn't be here. I'm missing out on time. Especially right now. Especially for my two boys, man. It kills me. I haven't been…that thing right there it eats me alive because I know. When I get out of here I have to relay that to them that I'm sorry about that. I'm going to do better, I'm not going to try any more. Because I've said that twice already. Things should work out from there.

IER: Can you tell me what being a father means to you? What is a father?

U03: Well, what is a father? A father is more than a best friend. He is a friend, but it's more than a best friend. It's like a father is that person that you can go to in any situation. A father is a person that can accept anything as far as change. I think a father would just be your best friend. Your best friend. Your parents are your best friends. They are the ones that will be there for you. Regardless of whatever happens.

IER: You're going to be there.

U03: Right. I keep stressing that I'll be there. It just keeps coming out of my mouth like that.

IER: How much time did you get to spend with them?

U03: Every two weeks we'd go to baseball games, hockey. We go to their basketball and football games and stuff like that. We'd just go over to the house and just chill out. They just come over my house any time they feel like it. They just come knock on the door and "what's up" things like that.

Again, the disjuncture between beliefs and actions is significant. As the respondent suggested, it is imperative for a father to be present in his children's lives in order to influence them. Through the respondent's words, it becomes obvious that he was not "physically there" for his children, and hence he was not very successful at influencing them in a positive manner.

According to Furstenberg (1995), there are several factors that influence the production of a "bad dad." Almost all of the men in the Furstenberg (1995) study (described more fully in Chapter II) were reared in absent-father homes and "spoke of being emotionally undernourished by their biological fathers" (p. 134). The majority of the "biological father" respondents in the interview component of the current study were the sons of "Absent" fathers (n = 8; 67%) while the remaining respondents had paternal types of "Workaholic" (n = 2) or "Loving and Supportive" (n = 1). As articulated by the respondents in Chapter IV, being reared without a father often results in the men having "missing pieces," and while they may intend to do the right thing, they are ill prepared for the amount of time and energy that is required of a parent.

Many of the men in the Furstenberg (1995) study entered parenthood with little planning, expressing surprise that their partners were pregnant. Consequently, the relationship between mother and father is generally a fragile one, with little commitment to the relationship by either partner. Still many of the respondents in the Furstenberg (1995) study "placed a high value on lasting relationships, and many hoped to marry someday" (p. 137). As the young men and women searched for the ideal relationship, they commonly formed sexual partnerships with multiple individuals resulting in a single young man fathering children by several women (Furstenberg, 1995).

These same themes emerged among the "biological fathers" interviewed. The respondents' spoke of being unprepared for the birth of their children, and ill equipped to be a father. They often spoke of very strained relationships between themselves and the mother(s) of their children. Also, the "serial father" was evident in the current study, as several of the men had children to multiple women. The majority of these men had absent fathers, which resulted in the young men having no "model" to guide their adult behavior. Consequently, while the respondents knew, cognitively, what a good father should do, their personal backgrounds and the decisions that they made as adults, became obstacles to successful fulfillment of their paternal roles.

Drug addiction proved to be another obstacle that blocked the ability of some of the men in fulfilling their paternal role. The "addicted" fathers (n = 5) represent a subcategory of "bad dads." While there is overlap between the characteristics outlined above and this group (for example 3 of the 5 men were also "absent" fathers,) the features that distinguish these respondents is their addiction to drugs and the decay that results in the father-child relationship.

The frequency with which this malady appears in the interview sample may have been an artifact of the housing units to which the researcher was granted access. As mentioned previously, in Chapter III, two of the four pods at the large, urban jail were program pods. Thus, it is possible that drug offenders were more prevalent in the study population than would be found in the general population of the jail. Nonetheless, with the drug policies that have been in place in this country for the past two decades, drug offenders represent one of the fastest growing groups of offenders in our nation's jails and prisons (Beck et al., 1993).

There are various perspectives of drug usage, and some consider drug use to be a "victimless crime." However, what emerged from the interviews in the current study was the devastating impact that a father's addiction can have on himself, and his family. The following respondent is a 38-year-old father of four teenage children. He was living with his wife and children until about three months prior to his arrest. He reported that his wife had separated from him because of his drug use. The interviewer asked the respondent about the importance of the paternal role.

IER: On a scale of one to ten, how important was your role as a father?

U32: How important is it?

IER: Yes.

U32: Or how important was it?

IER: Both.

U32: On a scale of one to ten, how important it is is ten, but was it, I'd have to say a three.

IER: I appreciate your honesty. What is a father? What does that mean to you?

U32: The father is the strength of the family. He keeps the family together by his example. He should be a friend, a teacher, confidante, provider, a friend. I said a friend twice. That's what I think a father should be. He should be approachable.

IER: What was your relationship like with your children prior to your incarceration, and prior to your separation. You can take it back as far as you want.

U32: It was good when I wasn't using. When I was clean, we had a great relationship. But then when I started using, the using would gradually take me away from them. And the stuff I would do, any family activities as far as I'm concerned, I wasn't included in them. I took myself out of them. I was not at no family functions. I broke promises, missed birthdays. I just wasn't a good father while I was using. Like I said, I think they still love me. I'm sure of it. I think they just want me to show them. So that's what it's all about. I made a lot of promises, didn't keep 'em.

The respondent was able to clearly describe his children's personalities and characteristics, and the activities that they enjoyed. It was obvious from his descriptions that he had been an involved or attentive parent at some point. The interviewer inquired about the strength of his relationship with his children prior to his arrest.

IER: How close were you to your children prior to your incarceration? Again, on a scale from one to ten.

U32: I'd say a five.

IER: Is that because of the drugs?

U32: Cause of the drugs, yeah.

IER: Okay.

U32: It was like I became...like I saw my kids while I was doing the things that I was doing. I was a shoplifter. I'd have to walk through the same area where my kids was and it was like I didn't have no shame or nothing. They would see me and stuff and their friends would see me carrying a bag of stolen goods. After a while everyone knew what I had. That just embarrassed them. It's an embarrassment. It took us further apart because when they'd see me coming they would try to act like they didn't see me and stuff like that. It was just terrible. Terrible.

IER: Earlier you described your mom for me and you described your grandfather. If I was talking to your kids and asked them to describe you, what words to you think they would choose?

U32: Hmmm. That's a good one. They might say I was selfish, cause I was. I don't know, my one daughter she told me she hated me. Not hated, she told me I wasn't her father one time cause they were really hurt. I would say they would say I was selfish. That says it all.

The next respondent is a 51-year-old father of two sons by two women, and the grandfather of one. He never lived with his oldest son, and lived only briefly with the youngest. He described his own father as a workaholic and a functional alcoholic. The interviewer was interested in what the respondent had learned from his parents.

IER: If you think about your parents again for a moment, what do you think are the most important things you learned from them about being a father?

U78: Probably commitment. I'm trying to think about what I learned from my dad and then did with my son but …responsibility. One of the biggest things that I learned now that come to mind, if I can't take care of myself, I can't take care of no one underneath me. So that's what I learned I think. If you can't take care of yourself, you can't take of no one underneath you. On the same token, if you don't love yourself, you can't love no one else…..I think that I probably learned from my mother that the man is the head of the household, nurturing from my mother. I learned how to keep a family together. Learn to respect my sisters and brothers. I learned to get along with my sisters and brothers and I learned to get along with other people too. I'm a believer that a lot things…that's where you get your first training…from your parents. No matter what you are, you are a product of your mother and father. You are a product of your environment to a certain extent. Like when I started messing around with drugs my dad owned a bar a liquor being legal. He looked at it like two different things. He told me, "I don't know why you mess with this shit (excuse my expression, that's just the way he called it). Because if drinking doesn't do it for me, I don't do it." He didn't know that addiction is addiction. My dad I don't think he even knew that he was an alcoholic because the only time that he would drink would be on the weekends. When he was taking care of business, he took care of business. But he drank every weekend. But he didn't want me using drugs on the same token. He didn't like it. I think they were more like ashamed of it or something. But it was alright to drink.

The respondent went on to describe the fragile relationship with the mothers of his sons, and his sporadic relationship with his children. The interviewer inquired about the importance of the paternal role.

IER: How important is it for you being a father?

U78: How important? Oh...

IER: On a scale of one to ten.

U78: How important to me is being a father. It's one of the most important things you can probably ever do in your life. Now whether you do it right or wrong that's two different things. To bring life into the world is an important thing. That's all you have. That's all the future is, is the kids. It's very important. I've been using drugs ever since I was 16. But I always managed to work and keep a job and all that. I think that I was a functional addict. But since I've been here I've been doing a lot of soul searching and a lot of thinking. Now I have a granddaughter now and a lot of things that I didn't do with my kids which I know some people say all for the wrong reasons and all that but to me as long as you are doing something good it can't be wrong. I'm saying I'm going to spend more time with my grandkids now. Try to do a lot of things for them that I didn't do for my kids.

IER: You said that being a father is important but if you do it the right way or wrong way. Did you do it the right way or the wrong way?

U78: I did it the wrong way. I'm the first to say it. There's been lots of times…I didn't spend a lot of time with my oldest kid. Lots of times I would take them to the park or something. We'd go out to [local amusement park] and I would say that I would pick them up at say 11:00 a.m. I'd leave my house at 10:00, I'd have to go get my dope. I'd go buy my dope and run around and do this, do this. I don't get there to pick them up until 5:00. Meanwhile their mother probably got pissed at me and then took them herself or something. Lots of things. My oldest was late probably for a lot of things. Missed out on a lot of things because…nothing came before them drugs. Even parenting, nothing.

IER: Can you describe to me what being a father means to you? What is a father?

U78: What is a father? What is a father? A father, in my eyes, is supposed to know everything. Which I didn't. A father is supposed to be there. Which I wasn't. What do I think a father is supposed to be…Like my father was. Good provider, show love and be there. I think that's the biggest thing I think is be there. You can buy a kid all the material things and don't be there for them and they'll turn to somebody else. They might get the wrong idea from somebody else. That was one of the biggest things when I was using. I didn't like to be around my kids because…I can remember one incident where my son was about 3 and it stopped me for using for about a year too. I was in the bathroom getting high and he come in the bathroom and opened the door. He was only three and he saw me and the way he looked at me. He was a kid but he knew that something was wrong. It really stopped me from using at home and I ain't going to say...cause I started using some place else. I really couldn't tell you. I can only tell you what a father should be like my father was cause he was there with me. I won't know because I've never really been a father. Selfish I guess.

IER: I asked you earlier to describe your parents and you did. If I was able to talk with your son, and asked him to describe you, what words would he choose?

U78: What would he say? I really don't have any ideas but he'd probably say that my dad was real busy. My dad was sick. That's what he calls guys that use drugs. He probably say...I really don't know. Honest to God. I don't know how he'd describe me.

IER: What do you think he'll learn from you about being a father.

U78: I think he is a better father than I was. His little girlfriend is going to college. I mean ex little girlfriend. He watches the baby while she goes to school. He's holding down a full time job. She'll bring the baby to his house and he'll watch the baby while she goes to school. He's crazy about his little girl. Just by doing that he's doing more than me. I was never a babysitter. I always paid someone. I never was a babysitter. But what he learned from me about parenting? Very little. I hope that he learned that you can't buy love. You can't replace material things for a real person being there. He learned how to be a man because he got to stand up on his own. I guess learn how to make decisions because I'm not there to make them for him. He has to grow up. My son by being raised by his mother and me not being there made him have to grow up very fast. I'm kind of lost and I'm thinking about that and I wasn't halve as good as father as I should have been.

Finally, the respondent below is 37-year-old stepfather of one daughter. His father was absent during his childhood and the respondent spoke candidly about the effect this had on him, and emphasized that he could never abandon a child because of this. However, his drug addiction resulted in that very outcome.

IER: What do you think are the most important things that you've learned from your father about being a parent.

U23: Nothing. Oh yeah, yeah, yeah, there is something. A lot of why I am today is because of him. Because I know what it is like to be a father. I know what it's like when Father's Day comes. You give your mother a call. Or you have father/son situation at school and you feel excluded from this. I know what it feels like. To be there for a son, daughter, whatever. You just can't be there but you have to be actively involved and show a genuine concern. If you don't show it, if you are just there just for the sake of it, then you are wasting your time. Because you have to show those kids that you are involved in what they are doing. You are showing a genuine interest. That's what excites them. To know that someone, hey, somebody cares. They have a recital and you are there and you are the loudest person in the audience. We all need attention and especially a child.

IER: So if you think now, again, both your mom, dad, the things that they've done for you and the things that they didn't do. You have said your dad wasn't there for you. Now if you think of yourself as a parent. How have you as a father been influenced by your mom and dad?

U23: Like I said...By me being from such a large family. We didn't get too much personalization. You know.

IER: I know.

U23: That hinders a lot. It did as far as the relationship with my mother because I felt isolated, but in the same token I realize that you can't do this. You have to…each child you have to deal with them individually and set times. Like, what's going on with you? And what's going on with you? You can't have favorites. They always do, but you shouldn't show it because we get jealous. I don't want any kids that I got thinking that he's better than the other. Your brother and sister and I love you both the same. I learned that from my mother. As far as my father, that role model…I can be separated from the mother but I don't think I would ever separate myself from the child. That's me. Whoever that child grows up to be is going to reflect on me. It would show whether I was a real parent or ….See a lot of people think that being a parent is just being sent your child support payment. That's not being a father. You might not want to say everyone but of course you got to take care of your child. A lot of people seem to think, "well I've paid my child support" and think that's it. But there's a lot more to it than that. How can you consider yourself being a father because you sent money every month and you might send a card on a birthday. C'mon. That's not what it is about. What it is about is, that's you. You wouldn't treat yourself no less than you would treat your son, so I mean, c'mon.

IER: They're a big part…

U23: You understand. We may fall back and need them. You've got to be there. Financially and physically and morally. It's a must. Because if you are not, you are fooling yourself and you are missing out on something. That's your problem. I just can't see another man raising mine. At all. He might be with the mother but still they are going to know who dad is. That you can't …fathers do but I can give that away. That's God given and we take that too much for granted. I don't because I didn't have a father. I want my child to have everything that I didn't have.

IER: When you were arrested, where you living with her? She and her mom?

U23: Yes and no.

IER: Can you explain that?

U23: When I started shooting, well I've been shooting hcroin for quite a while. But I stopped for almost ten years. What happened was this. During the course that I relapsed, I realized that I wasn't doing nothing but negative for me and I was bringing it around her and the kid. The mother was sick of it. I was sick of it and in all actuality I kind of realized that I was wrong for taking that around that child. So I left. It felt like the right thing to do. It also released me of any commitment that I had. I still periodically had to go around and say, hi. Seeing the child I would definitely acknowledge her and talk to her. "How are doing at school?" I felt bad because of the fact that I done what I was just telling you what I didn't want to do. Even though it wasn't my child. In God's eyes, that is my child because I accepted that responsibility and I turned my back. It was just that convenient, that easy of a decision. It's easy for me to say that but in all actuality it wasn't. I had a choice to make. Either to continue to do what I'm doing around her or not let her be a part of that, which is more important. At the time, my vision was all cloudy. My thinking was confused and I thought that that was more important. Now I realize different. You've got to understand something. Within the addiction of heroin, there are no sides. It's a very selfish thing that is focused on me. Bottom line is, if you got in my way at that point, you would be out and I would have to remove you in order to get...it's a physical addiction and you go through withdrawal symptoms. It's not a nice feeling. You do things that are maybe out of your character. I would like to think that no one is like that. Therefore, I felt that it was best, in the situation that I was in, that I just got away from them.

The fathers who were "bad dads" because of drug addiction reported a common "sequence" in the decay of their relationships with their families. First, the men expressed a belief that they could "balance" their drug use and their other responsibilities and obligations. As the drug addiction became more pervasive, there was a simultaneous erosion in important relationships, including the father-child relationship. As the respondents reported, all of their commitments to others (e.g. work and family) insidiously decayed to the point that they were willing to sacrifice everything to get high. Unfortunately, it is not until their addiction is under control that they can clearly see the cost of their addiction, and the impact of their selfish behavior on their family members, especially their children. Often this realization occurs inside the correctional institution, a place that is not conducive to healing the wounds of a broken family.

SUMMARY

The respondents in the current study had an average of 2.0 minor children, which is strikingly similar to previous studies of incarcerated fathers (Hairston, 1989; Beck et al, 1993). There was strong agreement among the respondents that the paternal role was an important one and the respondents clearly articulated what it meant to be a "good father." However, there was disjuncture between the beliefs and the actions of some of the interview respondents.

About one-half of the respondents in the current study were residing apart from their minor children prior to their incarceration and spent much less time interacting with their children than did respondents who resided with minor children. Most of the interview respondents who were absent from their minor children were the sons of "Absent" fathers and/or were addicted to drugs. In contrast, for the respondents who resided with their minor children prior to their incarceration, the paternal role was integral in their lives. Unfortunately, as delineated in the next chapter, incarceration adds further strain to the relationship between father and child.

CHAPTER 5

The Jail Experience of Fathers
Paternal Reactions to Separation from Children

"We who live in prison, and in whose lives there is no event but sorrow, have to measure time by throbs of pain, and the record of bitter moments." Oscar Wilde (1905)

Two of the central questions that this research project addresses are; (1) what is the nature and significance of contact with family during incarceration, and (2) do the pre-incarceration relationships of jailed fathers differentially affect the stress of incarceration. This chapter begins with an exploration of the nature and extent of contact between jailed fathers and their children.

FACE-TO-FACE VISITS AND OTHER CONTACT

The jailed fathers were queried about contact with their loved ones, in order to further explore the ways in which pre-incarceration relationships impact their term of incarceration. As outlined in Chapter 2, most of the studies to date on imprisoned fathers indicate that they have little face-to-face contact with their children (Hairston, 1989; Lanier, 1995; Hairston, 1995). The reasons for the infrequent contact include distance between prison and home, costs, and the pre-incarceration relationships that existed between the incarcerated men, their children, and the mothers of their children (Hairston, 1989;

Lanier, 1991; and Hairston, 1995). More specifically, fathers who resided with their children prior to incarceration (Lanier, 1991) and married fathers were more likely to maintain regular visits with those children during imprisonment (Hairston, 1989). In the Lanier (1991) study, nearly 72% of residential fathers had visits from their children. As mentioned in Chapter II, all of the aforementioned studies took place in prisons.

Because jails are typically located closer to an inmate's home than are prisons, it was anticipated that jailed fathers would visit more frequently with their children than imprisoned fathers. However, this was not the case. The results of the present study suggest that the jailed fathers had less frequent contact than did fathers from previous prison-based studies. As outlined in Table 14, while nearly 57% of the respondents whom resided with their minor children prior to incarceration have visited with their children in jail, a full 43% have had no visits. Similarly, only 41.3% of respondents who did not reside with their minor children prior to incarceration have visited with their children while jailed. The fact that jail inmates are physically closer to their families appears not to increase the likelihood of visits, although the inmates' pre-incarceration relationships do appear to influence contact with children during incarceration.

Table 14: Visits with Children by Parental Status

	Lived with all or some of their children (n=37)	Did not live with children prior to incarceration (n=46)	Row Totals
Children have visited	56.7% (n = 21)	41.3% (n = 19)	48.2% (n = 40)
Children have not visited	43.3% (n = 16)	58.7% (n = 27)	51.8% (n = 43)

Face-to-Face Contact: Parents and Mixed Parents

The interview data suggested various reasons for the lack of face-to-face contact between fathers and their children. Among interview respondents, 8 of the 13 men who resided with all or some of their children prior to incarceration reported that they preferred not to see their children in the jail. Several respondents indicated they had never visited with their children because they believed both they and their children would have a strong emotional reaction to seeing one another through a piece of glass. As these men recounted, it would be too painful to visit with their children and too painful for their children, thus they forego face-to-face visits.

The following respondent is a 42-year-old father of a 9-year-old son and 2-year-old daughter. The respondent indicated that he decided it would be best not to visit with his children.

IER: How long have you been here?

U36: Seven months.

IER: How often have you been able to see [son]?

U36: No. I don't want him coming here. We talk often.

IER: On the phone?

U36: Yes.

IER: What kinds of things do you talk about when you get him on the phone?

U36: The usual. Whatever special is happening he tells me. When are you coming home?

IER: You mentioned that you don't want him coming here to visit. Why is that?

U36: Mostly for me. I couldn't...it would be very, very, very hard not to be able to hug him. To look through him at the glass. I would feel...I would be hurt inside. I wouldn't want him to see me in this situation. Even though he knows that I'm in it, I wouldn't want to hurt him to see how devastated I am. Not to be able to hug him. Not to be able to touch him, be with him. Not be able to do things that we do. I just think that it's best left where it is. For his sake and mine.

The next respondent is a 50-year-old father of nine children, most of them adults. He was residing with his 7-year-old son at the time of his arrest. The interviewer asked him about their visits.

IER: Have you seen any of your kids since you've been here?

U31: No. No. No. I won't even put my kids on the list.

IER: Tell me why?

U31: I don't want to hurt myself like that. That hurts. It's bad enough that I am alone. But sitting here and seeing your kid outside that glass and you can't touch them that hurts too bad. I refuse to put them on my visitor's list. Any of my kids. Refuse to. When I get out I'll explain it to them. I feel like I'm doing it the way my parents would have did me. I just don't want to see them. I want to see them, don't get me wrong, but I don't want to see them in here.

IER: Under these circumstances.

U31: Right.

IER: If they came to visit, what would it be like for them?

U31: Emotional because I don't think that they could handle it. And I couldn't handle it either.

Other respondents decided to stop visits with their children after they experienced them. The following respondent is a 24-year-old father of five children. He was residing with four of his children at the time of his arrest. He had recounted to the interviewer his childhood memories of visiting his father in jail. The interviewer asked him about his visits with his own children.

IER: You told me that you've been here about six months. Have you seen your kids since you've been here?

U28: Once.

IER: You saw all of them? Or...

U28: [Names a son and daughter]

IER: The three and four year olds?

U28: Yeah.

IER: What was that like?

U28: Immediately my son noticed that always I don't ever want them to be down. So he comes in and says, "look daddy." He starts flexing his muscles and stuff. He goes, "look I can do pushups." He was just the whole time like making...like we have the phone up there so [daughter] and her mom's on this phone and he's on this phone and I'm looking back and forth like this. He's doing like this (gestures) and the people that's visiting next to me, he's making faces at them. Like man, you're silly. For the most part it was that distance in between. It was like there was a lot of distance in between us from being behind the window.

IER: Whenever I asked you about visits that you made at the old County jail to your dad, you said it was almost like a dream but maybe an unpleasant dream at that. Do you think that they have the same experience here?

U28: Yeah. Because my son was looking, he was on the phone and he came in and he's trying to talk to me and you can't hear through those big thick windows. He was looking at me like, "you're not going to say nothing?" I was like, "you gotta pick up the phone, man. You gotta pick up the phone." He picks up the phone, he looks, he's like, "hey dad." I looked at him, "what's up." He's like, "how come you're over there." He was like, "come over here." I'm like, "I can't man." That hurt. I had to sit the phone down for a minute. I laugh about it, but it hurt. I didn't want them to see me down because they are not used to seeing me like that. My daughter was even more, she was banging on the window, boom, boom, boom. The time went like that (snaps finger). That was the fastest hour I've had in my live. I never want to experience that again. I'm not going to let myself experience that again.

Finally, two of the respondents who resided with their children prior to incarceration indicated that the atmosphere that was present in the jail was not one they wanted their children to experience. The following respondent is a 30-year-old father of two daughters. He reported that he had made the decision not to visit with his children.

IER: You told me you've been here for about 6 months?

U39: Yes.

IER: How often have you been able to see your kids since you've been here?

U39: I haven't seen them.

IER: You haven't seen them.

U39: I haven't seen them at all, no.

IER: Why?

U39: It's hard enough for my ex-wife to come see me. She just came to see me. She hates this place. She hates the way she gets treated. She feels that she gets treated like a prisoner downstairs. Guards aren't all that, not all of them are friendly. Most of them aren't friendly at all. She just doesn't want to bring the kids into an atmosphere like that. Or, where they have to talk to me through, or upstairs they'd have to talk to me through a telephone. Some visiting booths have the speaker walls where the sound just comes through the wall.

IER: Do you think it would be too difficult for them?

U39: Yeah. She thinks it would be too difficult for them and too difficult for her in the process. I tend to agree with her. I'd love to see my kids and hopefully by the grace of God, I'll be in a program soon and I'll be able to see them for real, you know, instead of through a glass wall and talking through a telephone.

There were five respondents who resided with their children prior to incarceration and maintained contact through visits while they were jailed. However, none of these respondents were satisfied with the visits. In some instances, the physical design of the visiting quarters reduced the quality of the visit, from the fathers' perspectives. At the large, urban jail, inmates receive visitors on the second level of the housing unit. There are stools on both sides of a large glass window. Hence, the inmate simply moves to the second floor of the pod in which he is housed to visit with loved ones who remain physically outside the housing unit. This does not afford much privacy for the inmate and their family, as the following respondent reported.

IER: How long have you been here?

U33: It will be four months and maybe ten to twelve days. We'll give it an average, four and a half months.

IER: Have you been able to see your children?

U33: They've been here, yeah.

IER: How often do you get to see them here?

U33: Probably once a week. I get two visits a week. They visit once a week with their mother. Yesterday they were here. I got to talk to them about some things. We joked a little bit. I ask them about school. [Son] is really geared up. He's ready. He's very ready. They go to the same school now. This is going to be a challenge for both of them because they love to fight each other. They love to fight.

IER: When do they start school?

U33: I believe sometime in September. Hopefully I will be home before the start of the school year. I will feel less than if I'm not home with them. Because like I said, I take pride in doing their homework with them.

IER: What are the visits like?

U33: Here, well, just this pod alone I don't like the visits because it's too open, you know. The booths are just like, you pick up a phone and the only thing separating you is the glass. Compared to like upper levels, they have like a door, they are closed in. Like a little block space. You can talk through a ventilated, you know, window. You can't touch or nothing like that.

IER: If I understand, you might be sitting next to somebody who is having a visit and you can see everybody else. There's no privacy.

U33: Right. I don't like that. Everybody here, they look at your visits, like "wow, who is that?" It's uncomfortable that way.

The small, rural jail has a compact visiting area that looks like two telephone booths placed together with a common glass partition that is approximately waist high for an adult. There is a small shelf upon which one could lean, or perhaps place papers, etc. The area below the glass partition and shelf is constructed of bricks. Inmates speak to their visitors through a telephone. When small children visit they have difficulty seeing the inmate, and vice versa. The following respondent described visits with his wife and children.

IER: How often do you see your children?

R03: Three times a week. There was only three visits a week. My wife was here faithfully three times a week. You can ask those guards. They know her. They know my wife and kids better than they know anyone else who has ever been in here.

IER: I know that the visiting facilities are very small and you have nine children, so they can't all come once because they can't fit.

R03: No. And anyone that's 15 years and above uses up another visit. So my wife came and [oldest son] came, that's two visits gone. So [oldest son] wouldn't come as often. He would come when [my wife] would miss a visit or something. My daughter [gives name] is seventeen years; she doesn't want to come in here at all. She came one time and it really destroyed her to see me. The visiting booth is about that wide and it's on both sides. The glass is about that thick. You talk through a phone and half the time the people rip the phone apart.

IER: You have to stand up?

R03: All the time. See, that's the one thing we used to complain about. Why don't they put two stools on the other side. It's okay if we have to stand, why should they have to? They didn't ask for this. I used to tell my wife, why do you even come to visit. Cause it's hard on me. My two youngest

ones, my stepdaughters [names them], the window is like that.
There's a solid brick wall below the window, their heads come
to the top of the counter. They can't see me. My wife has to
put them up on the counter and then the guards yell because
they're sitting on the counter. They're afraid they'll fall and
get hurt and the jail would be liable. But they can't even see
me. They take the phone down and I don't even see where
they are standing. That part was hard on [names daughter].
She'd tell me, "it's hard, I can't even see you." My wife used
to try and hold them up, you know. She's got one on her
shoulder and then the other one wants to get up and she can't.
That's not fair to them. It really isn't. That's the one thing
that we complain about a lot out here. That's not right.

The following father reported feeling torn about continuing visits
with his daughters because of the pain the visits caused him and his
daughters. He is a 36-year-old father of four children. He was residing
with, and rearing on his own, his two youngest daughters. The
interviewer asked him about visiting with them.

IER: You've mentioned that you've seen your daughters.
How often have you been able to see them since you've been
here?

R11: They've been up about two times. And my mother she's
sickly and she can't get up here. My sister will only bring
them when she feels like moving. So she can't get up here as
much to bring them. I don't get that much contact with them.
Even on the phone I can't call them because my mother can't
accept collect calls. So I can't call. All I do is constantly be
wondering after 5:30, are they coming or what. What's going
on. That's the way it's been. The last time I seen them it's
been about three weeks now.

IER: What are the visits like?

R11: Well, it's heartbreaking.   It really hurts [youngest
daughter] a lot because she can't touch me, she can't hold me.

And when it's time for her to leave, she just falls all to pieces. [Older daughter] holds together and I mean I think she holds a lot of her inside of her. She holds a lot in her but [youngest daughter], she just breaks down. Because over the years [youngest daughter] has learned to cling to me so much. As far as the visits, I think they really hurt [youngest daughter] a lot but I think [older daughter] just holds hers in.

IER: Let me ask this, is it easier seeing them or not seeing them?

R11: I think for their sake and the way that this is, I prefer for them not to see me. If it's going to take and hurt them like this where I just visit with them for a half hour and then both are trying to talk to me on the little phone and passing it back and forth to tell me the little things that's going on in their life. I'd rather they wouldn't be disrupted and go on with their education and don't worry about what's going on with me. We'll be back together sooner than later so I don't know. But preferably no.

IER: You'd almost rather they not come.

R11: Right.

The important theme that emerges from discussions with fathers who resided with their children prior to their arrest and incarceration is that the jail environment is not conducive to the maintenance of the bonds between incarcerated fathers and their children. The "pains of imprisonment" (Sykes, 1958) includes for many of these men, choosing between the anguish that accompanies seeing their children through a piece of glass and the anguish of not seeing them at all.

Face-to-Face Contact: "Biological Fathers"

While the "parents" and "mixed parents" expressed reluctance to visit with their children, or displeasure with the visits, very few of the "biological fathers" expressed the same concerns. Of the twelve biological fathers interviewed, eight had not visited with their children, but only two of fathers expressed concern that visits would be too painful for themselves or their children. The first respondent is a 28-year-old father of one daughter. He reported that for the year prior to his incarceration he had seen his daughter "a couple of times." The interviewer asked about current contact with his daughter.

>   IER: How long have you been here?

>   U92: I've been here just for a month.

>   IER: Okay.

>   U92: I don't talk to her from the jail. I don't want her to come down here and see me in here, nothing like that. I don't want her going through that drama.

>   IER: How come?

>   U92: I just don't think that's a place for my kid to see me. She knew...I think she knew I was out there selling drugs and things like that. I wouldn't want her seeing me wearing this type of clothes. Seeing her without touching her. I can't see my daughter there without giving her a hug or a kiss. A piece of glass in front of me. If it was contact it would be a different thing. I'd rather smell my daughter, hug her and feel her and things like...I don't want to just look at her through a piece of glass. I'd rather talk to her on the telephone before I could see her.

>   IER: Other men expressed that exact same thing. It's too difficult.

>   U92: Too difficult for me.

The next respondent is a 37-year-old father of one stepdaughter. He expressed similar concerns about face-to-face visits being too painful.

IER: You've been here how long?

U23: Four months.

IER: Have you seen [stepdaughter] since you've been here?

U23: No….don't want to. I don't want her to see me in this situation.

IER: Why is that?

U23: I'm very emotional. It just makes me think how much I screwed up. How stupid I was. How stupid I am. The bad choices that I made. I already know about all that, I don't need to focus on that any longer. I need to focus on what's ahead of me. We write. We call. I call. And that's fine.

The other "biological fathers" who had no face-to-face visits cited other reasons for the absence of contact. In some cases, family members refused to bring their children to the jail. In other instances, the men had no contact with their children prior to their incarceration, and thus had no contact during incarceration. Interestingly, the four "biological fathers" who had face-to-face visits with their children had few complaints about the visits and suggested that their children were happy with the visits, as well. The following respondent is a 41-year-old "serial father." He has seven children by five different women. Four of his children are adults with whom he reported no contact. He reported seeing his three younger children on a weekly basis. The interviewer asked about those visits.

IER: What is it like for them coming here to visit you?

U89: They enjoy being here and talking with me. They just enjoy just being able to communicate with me. Tell me about my one son, the oldest one loves to tell me about his 64 games. His Sega 64 games or whatever it's called. Genesis Jet One it is. He tells me about how bad he's going to beat me playing when I come home. I can never beat him on none of those games. They try to make the best out of it. They don't come around here looking sad like, "dad I wish you could come home." They realize that I'm going to be here. Like the other day he asked me, "dad when you coming home to play me road rash?" So just to prepare him for whatever I told him, "when I get home you'll probably be 15 years old." He said, "five years? Wow!" I said, "well it might be." Which I don't think it's going to be that long but I'd rather tell him five years as opposed to telling him two and then I don't come home in two because he looks for what I say. If I say I'm coming home in two years, when two years are gone, he'd say, "dad you told me you were coming home. What'd you do?" So I told him that. He's alright with it. He's cool.

The next respondent reported visiting with his teenaged son and felt the visits were positive. He described how his younger son came to visit him on his own, but the older one has not.

U37: My son [name], I mean it's amazing; he's been down here about 5 times. He had to come down and they told him he was too early one time and he didn't have a ride and caught a bus and I'm looking at him like...I'm saying to myself, "why are you doing this when it's really a lot of trouble to come down here" and I really appreciated that. Our relationship right now, I'm thankful. I'm grateful that we are communicating because prior to my dad passing away, there was some friction there. And I don't blame them. They were upset. We weren't that close.

IER: You've mentioned that you've seen the younger son here? What about the older one?

U37: [Names son] hasn't been down. I talk to my mom a lot on the phone and I guess he gave my mom his phone number. He has an apartment. He lives down by [names town] now and he told my mom to give me the phone number but he also said that he'd be down a couple times and he didn't come down. So I guess I should take the phone number and call him and I haven't and he hasn't been down. But my mom tells me that he comes over and asks about me all the time. I don't know. I guess I'm being...I don't know...I'm waiting for him to come down. He's waiting for me to call and so I guess we are both acting like babies.

IER: How has being here changed your relationship with your kids?

U37: It's helped with [younger son]. These visits...we've had the greatest visits. These visits here even through the glass have been the greatest visits that we've had. We've had the greatest conversations. I know that may sound crazy but that's the way it is. I do all the asking and he likes that. I show all the attention. Not what's going on in here. It's not important what's going on in here. What's going on? How's he doing in school? Who's he dating? All those questions and we both cry up there. It's just wonderful. It's a great thing. So being in here, that wasn't happening. It's was so superficial out before I came in here because it's like, "what's up dad?" What's up?" And they know what's up right before I came to jail here. So it's been good, so I need to take it to the next step from here. What's the next step going be? Cause I can see that they're apprehensive and so am I. And so it's been good.

For the most part, the "biological fathers" did not report the same level of anguish with regard to visiting their loved ones, as did the men who resided with their children prior to incarceration. This is not surprising, given the limited or non-existent contact and weak emotional connection these men had with their children prior to their arrest. Consequently, when they received visits from their children, it caused little pain for these fathers, and they likely would not recognize that entering a jail for a visit has the potential to cause distress for their children.

Telephone and Other Contact

Many of the respondents reported maintaining contact with their children via telephone or by writing letters. Previous studies have suggested that a large majority of inmate fathers maintain regular telephone contact with their families (Lanier, 1991; Carlson and Cervera, 1992; Hanrahan et al, 1995). In the present study, telephone contact was more common than face-to-face visits for all respondents (See Table 15).

Table 15: Telephone Contact with Children by Parental Status

	Lived with some or all of their children (n = 37)	Did not live with children (n = 46)	**Row Totals**
Have spoken to children by telephone	75% (n = 27)*	63% (n = 29)	68.3% (n = 56)
Have not spoken to children by telephone	25% (n = 9)*	37% (n = 17)	31.7% (n = 26)

* One respondent failed to answer this question, thus n = 36

Sixty-eight percent of respondents who had minor children prior to their incarceration maintained telephone contact with them while jailed. A common complaint of nearly all of the interviewees was of the costs associated with making telephone calls. Most institutions do not permit incoming telephone calls, so inmates must place collect calls to their families, which can be expensive. The following respondent spoke directly to this issue.

IER: How often do you maintain contact with your children?

U28: Now I write them. Our collect calls are cut off because my girlfriend had to get a job and everything and she can't make that much money.

IER: The phone calls are expensive?

U28: Yeah. They're like $3 a call. If you just call and talk for like a minute it's $2.85. Calls are expensive. They're like $2.85 a call. That's crazy. Some places they got like calling cards that you can buy and use. These people are crazy here. They try to get you for all the money they can. For everything. That's crazy. They don't care about you staying close with your family. They figure, well, "you broke the law so we're going to punish you." I understand that. But there are guys that have kids and stuff that don't get to see their kids. And then like you are only allowed to make three phone calls a day. After the third phone call and you try to call again, it blocks your line and they have to call the phone company. If the phone company feels as though they don't want you to call, they make you pay money to get it turned back on to take the block off. That's crazy. I'm never coming back in this place.

The next respondent reiterated the same point; the cost of maintaining contact with family members can be prohibitive for many fathers.

IER: Okay. How else do you stay in touch with your children?

R05: Telephone.

IER: Okay. And we had talked before, for purpose of the tape, just how expensive using the telephone is.

R05: Oh my god. It's $2.35 to make the call and it's so many cents a minute. And I live long distance from here. And I'm not working. The price for me to see my kids, talk to my kids for a month, is no less than $200 a month.

IER: Is that including the visits here?

R05: That's including the visits and the phone.

IER: Okay.

R05: For what it costs for my wife to come here, sometimes she has to get a babysitter for the other kids, you gotta pay them. You can't expect someone to do something and not pay them. Umm...it costs me quite a some of money to be able to see my family. I bet we spent, I'd be willing to bet, $1,200 since I've come in here. Just on being able to see each other and talk to each other.

Aside from the cost, some of the fathers were not able to maintain telephone contact because they did not know their children's phone numbers. The following respondent discussed this.

IER: Are you able to speak with her on the phone?

U92: I don't know her phone number. Her mother's phone number and they don't receive collect calls at her grandmother's house. And I don't know the address. I just know where the house is.

IER: So you can't mail her.

U92: I don't know the address. I don't know the phone number, I just wish I could get the address or give her my number because I know that she'll write me. I wish it was possible.

Once again, the fathers who had limited or no contact with their children prior to their arrest, were less likely to use the medium of the telephone to maintain contact. However, for the fathers who were attempting to maintain contact, the costs associated with making telephone calls could be prohibitive.

IMPACT OF SEPARATION ON FATHERS AND THEIR CHILDREN

A man's incarceration has a significant, and most often negative, impact on his family members (Baker et al, 1978; Fritsch and Burkhead, 1981; Carlson and Cervera, 1992; Hanrahan et al, 1995), including his children (Johnston, 1995; Fritsch and Burkhead, 1981).

Fritsch and Burkhead (1981) suggest that children who were aware of their parent's incarceration often exhibited behavioral problems. Interestingly, the type of behavioral problems reported seemed to be related to the gender of the incarcerated parent. If a child's mother was incarcerated, the child displayed "acting in" behaviors (withdrawal, daydreaming, increased crying, etc) whereas if a child's father was incarcerated, the child exhibited "acting out" behaviors (hostility and aggressiveness, defiance, school truancy etc.). The parents reported "problems with their children in precisely those areas where they would traditionally accept major responsibility for the rearing of children if living at home" (Fritsch and Burkhead, 1981, p.86). Furthermore, inmates who had contact with their children both prior to and during incarceration were more likely to report the occurrence of behavioral problems among their children (Fritsch and Burkhead, 1981). The questionnaire data was examined to assess the jailed fathers' reports of the impact of their incarceration on their children.

Emotional and Financial Impact of Incarceration on Children

The fathers were queried regarding the impact of their incarceration on their children's well being. A total of 46 of the 83 fathers (55.4%) who have minor children reported that they had either noticed, or been told of, behavioral changes in their children during their incarceration (see Table 16).

According to the respondents, their incarceration has had both positive and negative influences on their children. The two areas with the greatest variation in reported behavioral changes were children's behavior at home and with their friends.

Table 16: Nature of Behavioral Changes in Children (n = 46)*

	Changes for the better	Changes for the worse
With friends	n = 13 (28.3%)	n = 20 (43.5%)
At home	n = 12 (14.5%)	n = 29 (63%)
At school	n = 15 (32.6%)	n = 17 (37%)
Grades	n = 14 (30.4%)	n = 8 (17.4%)
Involvement with CJS	n = 8 (9.6%)	n = 7 (15.2%)
Other changes	n = 9 (19.6%)	n = 11 (23.9%)

*Respondents could choose more than one category

Twenty-nine of 46 fathers (63%) reported that their children's behavior at home had worsened since their incarceration, which is not surprising. As reported earlier, 42% (n = 37) of the jailed fathers who had minor children lived with some or all of these children prior to their incarceration. The vast majority of these children were residing with their mothers, making the mothers solely responsible for their all facets of their children's care. Given the change in environment at home, it seems reasonable that some children would "act up" and that their mothers may be less able to handle their misbehavior given the extra burden they are shouldering.

The fathers were also asked about the effect that their incarceration has had on their children's emotional and financial well-being. The reports of the fathers who resided with children were compared to the reports of the fathers who resided apart from their children prior to incarceration. As shown in Figure 3, the fathers who resided with their children prior to their incarceration were more likely to report financial effects than were the fathers who resided apart from their children (54% to 42%). Additionally, one third of the non-resident fathers reported that their children's financial situation did not change as a result of their incarceration. These reports could reflect the non-resident fathers' lack of financial participation in the lives of their children prior to their incarceration. Importantly, not a single respondent reported that their children's financial situation had improved.

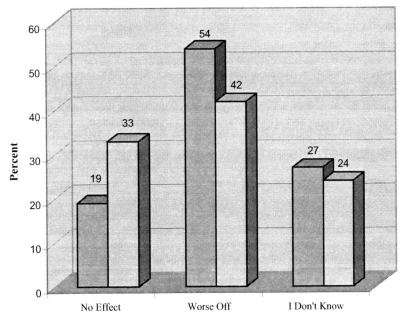

Figure 3: Financial Effect of Father's Incarceration on minor children
(n = 83)

| ■ Resident | □ Non-Resident |

Another area about which the fathers were queried dealt with the emotional response of their children. It was anticipated that the fathers would report much emotional distress. Thus, the respondents' reports regarding the emotional impact of their incarceration on their children were surprising. A large percentage of both resident and non-resident fathers (50% and 68% respectively) reported that they did not know if

their children were affected emotionally by their incarceration (See
Figure 4).

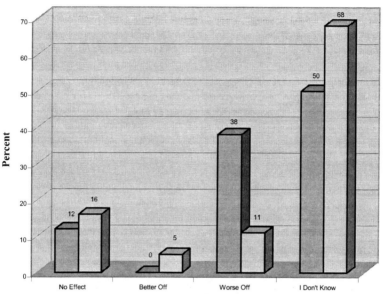

**Figure 4: Emotional Effect of Father's Incarceration on minor children
(n = 83)**

| ☐ Resident Fathers | ☐ Non-Resident Fathers |

Approximately 38% of the resident fathers reported that their
children were worse off emotionally as a result of their incarceration.
Also, none of the resident fathers believed that their children were
"better off" emotionally.

It seems possible that the questionnaire respondents were more
willing to acknowledge the financial burden that their incarceration
created and preferred not to acknowledge the possibility that their

actions caused emotional suffering among their children. An alternative explanation is that the fathers were less aware of any effect. The interview data suggests the former may be true, that questionnaire respondents were unwilling to admit the emotional impact experienced by their children.

Impact on Children – Perceptions of Parents and Mixed Parents

The interview data provides a different view of the perceived impact of a father's incarceration on his children. The majority (9 of 13, 69.2%) of the "parents" and "mixed" parents reported that their children had been affected emotionally by their incarceration. The emotional impact ranged from children not being able to interact with their father, to feeling shame or embarrassment about their father's incarceration, to believing their father did not want to live at home.

The following respondent is a 24-year-old father of four children and one stepchild. He was residing with four of his children at the time of his arrest. The interviewer asked him about the impact of his incarceration on his children.

IER: How has being here changed your relationship with your kids?

U28: Cause I'm not there at all in any kind of way. That's the one thing that I never wanted was to take myself away from my kids like I've done now.

IER: Because you kind of have an idea of what that's like.

U28: Yeah. I know what it's like. I can just look at my son and tell. He can play with his mom, but it's not like playing with me. He's a big dude. He needs me to play with him because I can kind of get rough a little bit with him. Wrestle with him and stuff. His mom can't do that. She can, but not like me. That's what he really need. That's what really keeps him calm. Me wrestling with him and stuff. That keeps him calmed down because he exerts his energy. Just running around the yard that don't really get nothing for him. My daughter likes to draw too because I do. Her and I are basically alike from living together I guess for so long. And then, I'm a role model to her. She wants to do some of the things that I do. She likes to draw and stuff. She brings me pictures, "[Name], can you fix this for me?" And I'll fix it for her. She'll look at me, "how come I can draw like this?" "In time you will, babe." It will come.

IER: What do you think your children have thought about you being here?

U28: They hate it. Even my youngest daughter she said, "daddy I'm mad at you." I said, "why?" She said, "because I can't give you a kiss." I said, "you can give me a kiss, I just can't feel it." That's the thing, the feeling. They can see me but they can't touch me. It hurts. My son was about to cry. I was like, "don't do that man, don't cry." I said, "I'll be home soon hopefully." Oh boy.

IER: How do you think you're being here has impacted them?

U28: It's changed them. They weren't the same when they came. When they figured out that they couldn't touch me, they were totally different. They came in all happy and stuff and when they seen they couldn't touch me, they were like, "what the heck is this?" This is nothing.

Another respondent described the emotional impact of his incarceration on his children, especially his sons. He is a 27-year-old father of five children. He was residing with all of his children at the time of his arrest.

IER: How has being here changed your relationship with your kids?

R05: It moves me out of the position of father. It moves me out of the position of protector. It moves me out of the position of enforcer as far as rules go. It takes a lot away from me and my children... [son] has asked me several times, "daddy why don't you come home?" "Don't you like me no more"? He's taking this personally. He thinks it's his fault. We all know it's not that. But he's too young to realize it. And I think, I think it's going to affect him, I really do. The kid is going to think that he's unwanted. The kid is going to feel that, you know, if my daddy don't want me, who will? And you can tell the child, you can tell him over and over again, "No [son] this isn't your fault". But it doesn't matter, it doesn't matter. They think that I want to be here, that I want to be away. And that's not good for them. I don't want my kids upset at me because of this. And even if I do go home, even if I...even if you were God and you could snap your fingers right now and I could home, my kids are still going to have these thoughts in the back of their head. You know, where was he? You know, to them I've been away a year. They don't know no better. Daddy's been away a long, long time. And it's going to be with them, it's going to stick with them. Why didn't daddy want to be here? You know. And now I'm stuck having to go home and sort all this out. It's pretty hard to explain to a three-year old and a five-year old what was going on. They don't want to hear it. So, you just do your best, you know.

A 42-year-old father of two spoke about his fear that his incarceration would result in embarrassment and shame for his son.

IER: Do you think that your incarceration has had any impact on him?

U36: I'm sure that it has. I was there every day and all of sudden I'm gone. It kills me when I think of his friends saying, "where's your dad?" And I know that [son] can't tell them "in jail." And it just...that bothers me more anything. To shame him. To shame him just crushes me. I feel very guilty about that. I wish it didn't happen and I'm going to do my best and pray that it doesn't ever happen again. To put him in this situation. But if I know [son], we will get past this.

Although once I am out of here, we are going to talk about this. And we are going to get it on the table and if he has any problems or resentments, I want to hear them. I want to get this as straight and clear as we can. I made a mistake. I paid for it. "You didn't make no mistake [son], but you still had to pay for it and I'm sorry." I'll let him know that I'm sorry and there is nothing else I can do. I can't replace the time I missed but the time we have now is what we got to work with. I'll explain all that to him. I'll ask him, "tell me what you want to ask. Do you want to scream at me? Do you want to punch me?" I'll get it out of him. Even it it's pulling teeth. I will do that. Like I said, we communicate

The next respondent discussed how his incarceration has left a void in the lives of his two daughters.

IER: How does being here change your relationship with your kids?

U39: How has it changed my relationship? Well, I can't be there to show them physical or financial support. If the youngest falls down and bruises her knee or cuts her knee, you know, or something, I can't be there to put a band-aid on it or whatever. If my youngest is having a problem with a friend or something, I can't help explain to her what she might be able to do or how she might be able to handle it or anything like that. But then again, can still talk about stuff on the phone with the oldest. I think the youngest, my youngest, she has really become like a complete terrible two. Although she just turned three you know. She was starting to get a little bit, you know because of me being with her everyday, she was just, you know, calmer. You know what I mean? And now it's my mother, or her mother, or a babysitter. Whereas everyday she had the stability there. Her life was in order, you know, our lives were in order, had an order to them. Now it's more chaotic, so I think me being away has definitely been detrimental to my youngest, you know as far as raising her up.

Because, you know, that at that age it is very important to have a regular parental unit there with you all the time.

IER: The oldest one understands that you are here. What does she think about that?

U39: Well, she's known pretty much since she was younger that I had a substance abuse problem. Of course, you know, dad's sick. But dad's only sick when he's in jail or when he's using. The rest of the time dad's all right. So, she, you know...I've been in other programs and they've never been for long extended periods of time, you know. She accepts it. It's not like she doesn't...it really saddens her a lot. My wife says that a lot of times she'll just all of sudden breaks down and starts crying, missing me and wanting me to be home and things like that.

IER: So, overall you'd say that you're incarceration has had a pretty big impact on them.

U39: Yeah.

Other effects reported by the "parents" and "mixed parents" included behavioral changes such their children "not listening" to adults (n=4) or having problems in school (n=2). The first respondent is 22 years old and was residing with his girlfriend, her two children and their child. He discussed behavioral changes in his three year old.

IER: How has being here changed your relationship with your kids? They're pretty young but do you think that it has changed your relationship?

U64: The last time my daughter came down here she doesn't listen to me like she used to when I was there. Kids are smart. When she comes to visit she knows there is a glass. She knows that I'm on one side so she knows there is nothing I can do to her. I tell her to have a seat, sit down. She tells me, "no." She never done that before. Those kinds of things.

IER: She's three. Kids go through that stage where they say "no" to everything. That's their first response. Do you think that is part of her age right now?

U64: No. She's bad. She's terrible. She gives her mother a hard time. So she's definitely changed.

IER: Do you think that is because she's growing up and going into that stage or because of this situation?

U64: Probably this situation.

IER: How else do you think your incarceration has impacted your kids?

U64: There are just certain things. Their mother doesn't have patience like I have. They need me there. My stepson, I taught him how to ride a bike. And I taught my daughter how to ride a bike, and her oldest daughter. She [girlfriend] doesn't have the patience to teach the kids how to ride a bike. She doesn't take as much time as I do with the kids to help them with those things. They really need me there.

The following respondent described how his children have "lost trust" in him and have suffered in other ways, as well.

IER: How has being in jail changed your relationship with your kids?

R03: They've lost a lot of trust in me to because I can say I'm not going back to jail and I could say you don't have to worry. It's still a doubt in their mind. I see it. Because you know when you tell a kid something and they look away. I see it in quite a few of their faces. The trust is the biggest thing and I feel like I let them down because I wasn't there. Like with son] getting in trouble, if I was there, I don't know if I could have stopped it. But he probably would have talked to me about it a little bit more and maybe I could have deterred it, you know. Or it wouldn't have been as bad as it was. Like my daughter [name], her grades have sunk an awful lot. They were real, real good. [Wife's name] has only like a ninth grade education and school has changed a lot from when she was a kid and when I was a kid till now. Kids have computers and everything. I try to keep up with it as much as I can. We have a computer at my house for the kids. I learned the new tricks for algebra and stuff and try to help [son] with that. He just doesn't grasp it. But, that's the thing that they are missing. I feel like I let them down a lot by coming in here. It was my own stupidity. That's basically what it was though. The trust and you know, I did let them down a lot.

In sum, the "parents" and "mixed parents" identified emotional and behavioral effects as being prevalent among their children. None of the fathers who resided with minor children prior to their incarceration reported positive effects resulting from their incarceration. Erosion of the father-child relationship concerned these fathers and they were cognizant that their incarceration was a source of emotional strain for their children.

Impact on Children – Perceptions of Biological Fathers

Interview data from the "biological" fathers reveals reports of a different nature. First, two of the fathers had no contact with their children prior to incarceration and no contact during their incarceration. Consequently, these respondents were not aware of any effects of their incarceration on their children. The words of the following respondent reflect this point.

IER: How long have you been here?

U93: Four months.

IER: Have you seen any of your children since you've been here?

U93: No contact.

IER: Has being here changed your relationship with your children or not?

U93: They are getting older now. So what's stopping them from dropping a $1.75 and getting the transfer and coming down and see me. But if I started thinking like that and living off that I'm being selfish. So being that I ain't played no part that's the results that you get. And I don't like it so being they are like that, I got to change. So I know what I got to do. I pretty much understand what I got to do.

IER: Do your children know that you are here?

U93: I imagine so.

IER: But you are not sure. What do you think that they think about it?

U93: Yeah. The three of them know.

IER: Three of them...the older ones?

U93: The older ones. What do they think about it? I couldn't even really begin to tell you but I know that there is another year gone. "Oh yeah. Okay." They sigh and move on.

Two other "biological" fathers were not sure of the impact that their incarceration had on their children. These fathers were seeing their children infrequently (weekly or less) prior to their incarceration. Perhaps because of the infrequent contact, these respondents were not certain of the impact, if any, of their incarceration on their children.

The following respondent is a 34-year-old father of two sons. Both boys were residing with aunts, and the oldest son was living out of state.

IER: How has being here changed your relationship with your children?

U22: A lot because I don't get to see them.

IER: What do you think your kids have thought about this?

U22: They love me so much I don't think they are too much upset. But as far as their mother...she's been in this situation a lot more than I was so it's hard for them to deal with. Because she's been in and out of their life but I was there a lot for them. They probably understand that I was trying to do my best to take care of them.

IER: Do you think that this has had any impact on them?

U22: They've been through so much. [Youngest son] was premature he was only this big (gestures). He suffered a lot when he was little. [Oldest son] too much don't bother him. You've got to see him. He's doing well. I write him, send him cards now and then. He wrote me. He's on the honor role. He's very happy and pleased where he is.

Six of the remaining eight "biological" fathers identified that their incarceration had a positive impact on their children. Three of these respondents reported that their incarceration had a permitted increased contact and communication with their children, and an opportunity for rebuilding their relationship. The following respondent spoke about the positive communication that occurred between he and his son during visits.

IER: Do you think this is going to have any kind impact on them?

U37: I think that I can have a positive impact.

IER: How so?

U37: Because it can be a starting point. It can be a starting point to a new relationship. This has been a blessing to me actually being in here. It's been a blessing to me, it really has. I needed to come in here. There was no way I could stop through my own devices. I wasn't going to stop. I couldn't. The bad heroin addiction and then cocaine. It's tough and I wasn't going to stop. So I was forced to stop and I'm thankful. I'm 45 and still have my health and they see it that way too. Because they know, like I said, they're not young. They know. I didn't hide that. I can't sugar coat that in any way with them. I think they were relieved too that I came here. They were relieved. And so I can be positive in the fact that I'm really determined to do what I need to do for myself. And by doing that for myself, I just believe that our relationship will get better. So this could be a starting point. That's the positive thing that I see out of it. I don't think I should be in here too much longer. I think I'll be out this year around Thanksgiving or something. So that can be a positive thing. As long as I take the next step and do what I need to do.

Three of the "biological" fathers believed that their bad decisions and subsequent incarceration would serve as examples for their children, and would prevent them from making the same mistakes. The following respondent is a 45-year-old father of one son. He reported that he had sporadic contact with his son throughout his son's life. The respondent indicated that he had no contact with his son while incarcerated.

IER: How do you think your being here has impacted him? What do you think the impact is going to be?

U38: Hopefully for the good. I used to kid around with him all the time. In fact I used to have t-shirt that says, "I'm not totally useless, I can always serve as a bad example." I used to tell him that all the time. I said, "look [son] you see where your dad goes wrong, I run with the wrong people and the drugs. Do you see what they do to me and my life?" As far as

I know, like I said up until last Christmas when we was still talking and tight and shit before I really went off the deep end, I mean the kid wouldn't even touch a cigarette. Wouldn't touch a beer. So in a way, my screwed up life, I think, has had a good impact on him in a way. It's a hell of a way to make an impact. (Laughs) He has looked at what has happened to me. In a round about way, I think it had a good impact on him.

The final two "biological" fathers reported that their incarceration had a negative impact on their relationship with their children as it served to further erode an already fragile relationship. Still, they were not able to identify the way in which their incarceration affected their children's emotional state. The following respondent is a 23-year-old father of three daughters by three different women. The interviewer asked him about the effect his incarceration had on his children.

IER: Do you think your being here has had any impact on your children?

U29: Yeah. I think it did. Specially, my oldest daughter [names her]. Because we already wasn't close all like that. And shoot, I've been here almost a year. That dragged what little bit of a relationship that we had away. Same with [other 4 year old daughter] maybe. She still admires me, talks to me in the same ways but I'm pretty sure that I'm going to have to build our relationship that we had back up. Cause I was all that she talked about before. "My daddy gonna do this, my daddy gonna do that." People be telling me when I'm not around that all she talks about. My mom says she talks about me but I'm pretty sure I'm going to have to some building again. Just like with my youngest daughter too. Like I said, she acknowledges me, jumping up and getting excited when I came around but I'm pretty sure when I get out of here it's going to take some time for her to know to me. For her to know that I'm the dude that's going to be there. I'm going to be there. Like when you wake up in the morning, I'm going to be there. When you go to bed at night, I'm going to be there. I'm a part of your life just like your mom is. Like you've been with your mom everyday, you're going to see me everyday now.

IER: So you have some work to do.

U29: Yeah. That's right.

In summary, the interview data suggest that the men who resided with their children prior to their incarceration were much more cognizant of, and concerned about the impact of their incarceration on their children. Nearly 70% of the "parents" and "mixed parents" reported that their children had suffered emotionally because of their incarceration, and 50% reported changes in their children's behavior at home and/or at school.

Conversely, the respondents who resided apart from their children at arrest did not report emotional or behavioral problems among their children. Understandably, some of these respondents had no contact prior to their incarceration and no contact during their incarceration, so it would be unlikely that their incarceration would influence their children. However, the respondents who did have contact with their children prior to their incarceration were no more likely to report emotional or behavioral changes in their children. It seems plausible that these respondents chose to "not see" the negative impact of their incarceration on their children, or to put a "positive" spin on the situation, such as the respondents who believed they could serve as a bad example. An alternative explanation is that these respondents are not "attuned" to their children, thus they do not make note of their children's suffering.

Impact of Incarceration on Fathers

In order to examine if the stress of incarceration is different for fathers who resided with children prior to their arrest, it is first necessary to understand the prevalence and nature of the stress the jailed fathers experienced during incarceration.

As outlined in Chapter 2, correctional facilities have unique environmental conditions, such as loss of freedom and rigid structure and rules, that can be significant sources of stress for those confined

(Johnson and Toch, 1988; Gibbs, 1986; 1987; 1991; Toch, 1992; Lindquist and Lindquist, 1997). Additionally, incarceration results in separation from loved ones, but this is not unique to the environment of the jail, as many individuals are separated from their loved ones due to work, military commitments, or family arrangements (e.g. separation and divorce) but the separation is different, in part because of the shame and stigma associated with incarceration (Goffman, 1961). Thus, one obstacle faced in this study was separating the stress that was caused by the jail environment from that which was caused by separation from family. The information presented in the prior chapter indicated that "parents" and "mixed parents" spent more time interacting with their children, and had stronger relationships with their children prior to incarceration, than did the "biological fathers." Because of this, it was anticipated that the "parents" and "mixed parents" would have higher levels of stress than the "biological fathers," due to the abrupt severance of the father-child relationship that occurs with incarceration.

As detailed in Chapter 3, a "supply-demand congruence model" was used to measure the jailed fathers' environmental needs and their perceptions of the availability of necessary resources in the jail environment (Gibbs, 1991; 1987). The Jail Preference Inventory (JPI) was used to measure environmental need and a shortened version of the Environmental Quality Scale (EQS) was used to measure supply of resources. Finally, the "emotion index" measured the frequency of negative affect reported by the respondents.

Reliability of the Jail Preference Inventory

The coefficient alpha was computed for each of the Jail Preference Inventory (JPI) scales (see Table 17). The reliability coefficient provides a way to determine if the scales are giving a true score for the particular concern or dimension. The reliability coefficients indicate that five of the seven scales are sufficiently reliable for research purposes.

Two of the scales, JPI Autonomy and JPI Safety, have decent internal consistency while three other scales, JPI Activity, JPI Privacy and JPI Support, have only very marginal internal consistency, indicating considerable error variance in these measures (Nunnally, 1967).

Table 17: Reliability Coefficients for the Jail Preference Inventory (JPI)

Environmental Concern	Coefficient Alpha	N
Activity	.49	n = 74
Assistance	.29	n = 79
Autonomy	.79	n = 83
Certainty	.06	n = 79
Privacy	.56	n = 74
Safety	.75	n = 77
Support	.62	n = 72

The final two scales, JPI Assistance and JPI Certainty, have so much random error associated with them that they will not be used in subsequent analysis. As reported in Chapter III, these scales had considerably higher reliability in previous studies (Gibbs, 1991; Gibbs and Hanrahan, 1993; Lindquist and Lindquist, 1997).

Inter-Scale Correlations for the Jail Preference Inventory

Table 18 presents the inter-scale correlations for the JPI. The predominance of negative associations is likely a result of the comparison-by-pairs format of the instrument. The magnitudes of the correlations indicate that the JPI scales are independent. The dimensions that show the strongest negative correlations are Autonomy and Support, and Autonomy and Safety, and the dimensions that show the strongest positive correlations are Autonomy and Privacy. Conceptually, it seems logical that these scales are related in this way.

Table 18: Correlations Between Jail Preference Inventory Scales (JPI)

	Environmental Concern			
Environmental Concern	Autonomy r (p)	Privacy r (p)	Safety r (p)	Support r (p)
Activity	-.13 (.28)	-.11 (.38)	-.34 (.005)	-.05 (.66)
Autonomy		.44 (.00)	-.56 (.00)	-.64 (.00)
Privacy			-.37 (.001)	-.46 (.00)
Safety				.30 (.011)

Paternal Type, Environmental Congruence, and Stress

The conceptual framework for the measurement model used leads to the prediction that the more an individual's needs are met by his environment, the less likely he is to experience stress in that environment. Conversely, if an individual's needs are not met by his environment, stress will result and will be reflected by a heightened negative emotional response (Gibbs, 1987; 1991; Gibbs and Hanrahan, 1993). It was also predicted that the jailed fathers who were parents would experience increased levels of stress, because of separation from their family, which is independent of environmental concerns.

The combined measure of need and supply that best reflects the model proposed by Gibbs (1987; 1991) and permits measurement at the interval level is to compute a "need" by "perceived supply" interaction variable (JPI X EQS) for each environmental dimension. This represents a "demand weighted supply" score for each respondent. These scores are then added together to determine a " Total Environmental Concern Interaction Score" (TECIS) for each individual (possible range = 1 to 600).

Each individual's parental status was categorized as either (1) a parent; (2) a biological father; (3) a mixed father; or (4) other. These categories were based on the fathers' reports on the questionnaire regarding with whom they resided prior to incarceration. As detailed earlier, the interview data revealed some validity problems with this categorization of the fathers. However, the interview data did confirm that most of the men who self-identified as "living with no children," had much less contact with their children than did men who self-identified as "living with" their children. This is not a perfect measure, but it does adequately capture differences in prior father-child relationships.

The "parent" and "mixed" categories were collapsed, for the following reasons. First, the interview data revealed that there are no significant differences between these two groups. While the "mixed" group did not live with all of their minor children, they lived with some of their minor children prior to incarceration. The impact of the separation was no less traumatic for these fathers because they lived with only some of their children and not others. It made sense conceptually to combine these two categories. The "other" category was dropped from the analysis because this group consisted of respondents who had either (1) all adult children (n=5), or (2) children who were born during the respondent's jail sentence (n=4). Thus, these individuals were not residing with any of their children prior to their incarceration for reasons outside of their control.

The Total Environmental Concern Interaction Score (TECIS) and the "parental status" variables were regressed on the dependent variable, the "emotion index." All of the results were non-significant. Upon consideration of the findings, it is believed that they resulted from problems with the measure, in this case the "supply" measure. There was more variance in 6 of the 7 dimensions of the supply measure than was present in the need measure (JPI), which was unanticipated. It seemed logical that individual "needs" would vary greatly among respondents, but that there would be less variation in their subjective ratings of the resources available in the jail environment. This was not the case. The supply of each environmental commodity was measured by a single item using a 10-centimeter line response format. For reasons that are not clear, many of the respondents placed the slash at one of the two extremes, which resulted in more variation in the supply measure. It is possible that the variation in the supply measure reflected environmental differences between jails, or between housing units at the large, urban jail.

Further analysis was completed using the "emotion index" and the "parental status" variable. As outlined in Chapter III, the emotion index consists of four items that question how frequently respondents experience (1) anxiety, (2) depression, (3) loneliness, and (4) anger. Each item was measured using a 10-centimeter line response format. The emotion index was "unbundled" and the "parental status" variable was regressed on each of the four negative affect items (anger, anxiety, depression, and loneliness). The results for three of the regression analyses were non-significant (anger, anxiety, and depression). The results of the regression analysis of "parental status" and "loneliness" are presented in Table 19.

As can be seen in there is a statistically significant difference in the frequency of loneliness reported by the fathers. In this sample, the men who resided with some or all of their minor children prior to incarceration reported higher frequencies of loneliness than did men who resided apart from their children prior to incarceration.

Table 19: Regression of Loneliness on Parental Status

Variable	Unstandardized Regression Coefficient (b)	95%Confidence Interval		Beta
Parental Status	-1.46	-2.69	-.250	-.26

$R^2 = .0664$ F = 5.77*

*Significant at a .018 level

Emotional Impact – Parents and Mixed Parents

The interview data of the respondents who resided with children prior to incarceration provide further evidence of the negative emotions experienced by the jailed parents. This was an area where the interviewer often had to prod the respondents, as they seemed reluctant to report on their own feelings regarding separation from their children. The interviewer was interested in both (1) how the respondents felt about being separated from their children – their emotions, and (2) how the respondents coped with being separated from their children – their actions.

The emotional reactions of these respondents varied.   Three respondents reported feeling "angry" at themselves, or "anger" toward the criminal justice system. Three respondents reported that they "felt like crap" because of the anguish they have caused their children. Six respondents reported feeling "very hurt" or "torn apart," and powerless to change their situation. One respondent was unable to articulate his feelings regarding separation from his children.

The first respondent was angry at what he considered an "unjust" system. He was incarcerated for failure to pay child support to his two older children who resided with their mothers. Interestingly, this father was raising his two youngest daughters on his own and received no support from their mother. He described the difficulty he had in trying to support four children on a limited income.

> IER: Okay. You told me a few minutes ago that the three most important things that a father does for his children are provide for them, teach them right from wrong and encourage them about making sure they get a solid education.

> R11: Right.

> IER: Have you done those things for your children?

> R11: As best as I could I can honestly say as best as I could. I mean for the children that I have and having the two with me and what the courts wanted for child support plus me taking care of these two is virtually impossible me doing it by myself. And the way the job situation is around here and getting the type of money that you need to take care of a family it's virtually impossible. That's why I've always wound up with contempt of courts because I just couldn't afford it. I believe in one point in time I had to pay $497 a month but then when I'm only making about $1,100 a month plus trying to pay the rent and all the utilities and I lost my home and having these two girls, lost two places already. It's virtually impossible.

> IER: You're actually supporting all four of them.

> R11: Yes. And it's impossible. It really is on my income. And when I ask them can they lower it I get so much hassle. A lot of hassle. I think women got it more easier getting things done. I said I had this big responsibility with them two girls and raising them and I've been literally dogged. I mean literally dogged. I don't get no help. There's not much I can say on that. But it really makes me mad.

The interviewer also asked the respondent, how being apart from his children made him feel.

IER: Being away from them, being physically separated from them, how does that make you feel?

R11: Really mad. I mean it does. It really does. Just like I said, I don't judge nobody for what they've done but if I was a real common criminal and I was here on something that I did wrong I guess it would be a different situation to judge it. But being here the way I'm here, what I'm here for, it just totally blows me out of the water. I'm just pissed off. Let's put it that way.

The following respondent is the father of two children. He was residing with his daughter prior to his incarceration, and was solely responsible for raising her. He had limited contact with his son who resided with his mother out of state. The interviewer asked the respondent how he felt being apart from his children.

IER: How does it make you feel?

U85: It makes me feel bad. I feel like shit. I feel like they're paying for my past. It ain't fair to them. It ain't fair to them. I wish things could be different now but everything happens for a reason and I believe that something good is going to come out of this no matter what happens. I know that I'm going home and that's all that matters and I'll never do nothing to jeopardize me not being able to be with my kids again. Especially my daughter. There's nothing I'll ever do to leave her again.

The next respondent is a 24-year-old father who resided with his girlfriend, their 3 children and her child from a previous relationship. He had previously described the jail experience as feeling like a "dream."

IER: How have you dealt with being apart from your kids? I guess first let me ask, how does it make you feel?

U28: Like crap. I think about them all day, every day. I try to go in my room and read my bible or read a book to stop thinking about it. Or write them a letter. It doesn't help though. It drives me crazy not to be with my kids. When they are waking up in the morning, usually I'm giving them breakfast and then I'm going to work. When I wake up here, I'm in that cell and it's wild, it's crazy.

IER: Still feels like a dream.

U28: Yeah. Definitely. Worse than a dream. It's like a nightmare. A bad, bad, bad, like a Freddie Krueger nightmare.

Another respondent also spoke of the pain that he experiences being apart from his children. He stated that not only was he suffering, but so too were his wife and children.

IER: How has all this made you feel? How do you feel being apart from your kids?

R05: It sucks. It really sucks. There is nobody, not even my wife, no one in my life that I love more than my children. Nobody. I would kill or die for my kids. If it boiled down to that then that's what would happen. I would kill or die for my wife if need be but I would be quicker to jump for my kids. My wife can fend for herself if she has to. Those five babies can't. And if I'm not there for them, who is going to be? I'm their dad. This system has taken away basically the only sense of security that my children have.

IER: Okay. How does all this make you feel?

R05: It tears me up. It tears me up. What tears me up most is that my hands are tied. I can do nothing about it. If I had the choice and I chose to be away, it would be different. But given that I was so rudely ripped away from my family and am now being held hostage away from my family, it tears me up. It does. You know I'm a full grown man but it's not beyond me to tell you there are times I lay up there in that bed and I want to cry. I think of my kids. I want to go home. And... there are times I lay up there just want to cry. There is nothing I can do. My hands are tied.

The final respondent is a 30-year-old father of two daughters. He described the void in his life that accompanies being apart from his children.

IER: I'm especially interested in how you deal with being away from your kids.

U39: I'd say, I don't know. Just think about what it's like being away from your kids for a long period of time. I know when I used to work and I'd go out on the road for a week or two weeks, you know. That was hard. You know. Even when I was in my addiction, you know, and I'd be gone and I wouldn't come home at night. That was hard being away from them. I don't know. I don't sleep very well at night. We have the family bed thing going in our house. Everybody sleeps in the king-size, both me and my wife and the two girls. So, it's comfortable. I don't sleep as good as I used to. Trying to fill the void of what it's like, you know, of having someone look up to you. Needing you.

IER: How does it make you feel?

U39: I feel like I've abandoned them maybe. Feel like I'm causing a lot of pain and suffering in their life that is completely unfair to them. It's not right for them, what I did. I guess I feel a lot of ...what would the word be... I get angry with myself a lot. For not being there for them.

Coping Strategies – Parents and Mixed Parents

The coping strategies of these respondents (n = 13) can be broken down into three categories. The first strategy was "keeping busy." Six of the respondents spoke of reading, writing, identifying goals, participating in programs, etc. as a means to avoid focusing on being apart from their children. The following exchange highlights this reaction.

IER: How have you dealt with being apart from you kids?

U01: Read. Read a lot. Look at their pictures. I got their pictures on top of my cabinet. I keep them out. I don't think about it. When you are locked up you can't think about it because if you think about it, it will drive you crazy. When I'm sitting here thinking my 13 year old daughter is out there having sex and by the time I get out there she'll be pregnant or something like that. That will drive you nuts. Or [son], 10 years old and getting sent home from school everyday because he's fighting. Getting kicked out of school. Or [younger daughter] not even making it to school. With her mother not even making to school. I'd go crazy. So when you come to jail you start to…you don't think about things that you can't control. You try to forget about the outside world because you are in the county jail. You'll be there soon. You haven't killed anybody, you're not going to be gone forever. Really you don't think about it. You read books. At least I do. You try to take yourself to another fantasy world. A book or sports. You play basketball. You tire yourself out and you sleep and you don't' dream. It's tough too. It's tough.

Another respondent also described "keeping busy" as a way of dealing with being separated from his children, especially his daughter.

IER: What have you done while you've been here to deal with being apart from her?

U85: Anything that I can. I go to school in here. I got my GED in here. I've done everything that this jail has to offer.

There isn't one thing that I haven't done. There's nothing else for me to do. I've done everything in here. I've been in here so long. I did school already. I did everything. As far as the resources group thing, I've done everything in here. There's nothing else for me to do. These last couple of weeks I've been going crazy. Just trying...you know. Just talking to her is the only thing that keeps me going.

The second coping strategy identified by respondents was "turning to God." Four of the respondents reported that they had drawn strength from their religious beliefs in order to deal with the separation from their children. The respondent below articulated this strategy.

IER: This is something that I'm really interested in. How have you dealt with being apart from your kids?

U33: I had to look to God for that. Because emotionally being away from them, I'm torn apart inside. Very torn apart. I had to look for spiritual guidance to keep me from being so angry at either myself or others for my mistakes. I pray a lot about God taking care of my kids while I can't. To show them, support them, everything. And for me not being there to do those things, it's a serious blow. I don't wish jail on anybody. I wouldn't even wish jail on my worst enemy. For men that have kids, it's a hurt. It's a very deep hurt. It's a deep pain. If you love your children, it's a deep pain. I deal with it on a regular basis.

IER: What do you do with that pain? Or how do you deal with it?

U33: I give it to God because that's the only way I can deal with it. When I give it to him, the burden is lifted.

The final coping strategy for dealing with separation from children identified by respondents was "avoidance" or "acceptance." These respondents (n = 3) tried not think about being away from their children or tried to accept the situation because they could not change it. The following respondent spoke about the "avoidance" strategy.

IER: How do you deal with being apart from your daughters? What do you do?

R11: All that I do is sleep. When I first came in I didn't want to talk to nobody. I didn't want to bother with nobody. I just wanted to be by myself. Course, I've always been a loner all my life most anyway but I do actually just lay in bed and stare at the ceiling. That's all I do. There is really nobody that I really want to talk to here. Nobody else can help me with my problems but me. I feel that they couldn't tell me nothing that I don't know and they ain't got no solution for me so I just don't talk. I keep to myself. That's how I deal with it.

Another respondent clearly and concisely articulated his acceptance of an unalterable situation.

IER: How do you deal with being apart from your daughter?

U095: I don't deal with it, I just accept it. There's nothing I can do.

It is important point out that there did seem to be a correlation between coping strategy and placement. None of the rural respondents (n = 3) identified "keeping busy" as the strategy adopted to deal with separation. It is possible that there are fewer programs available for the inmates in the rural jail.

This study did not examine the extent to which loneliness and the other emotions experienced by jailed fathers, are related to problems within the jail. However, one of the respondents identified this link between separation from children and behavioral and emotional disturbances in the jail. The respondent was talking about society having greater awareness and recognition of the difficulties faced by incarcerated mothers than they do of incarcerated fathers.

R03: People understand what it does to kids and mothers and stuff outside. Nobody understands what it does to [fathers] in here. Fathers...it kills all of us. They don't see it from our perspective. They see it from the [perspective of the] ladies upstairs and how hard it is to be here, away from their kids. Fathers bringing their children over and they can't touch them and stuff. It hurts us just as much. It really does. I miss my kids a lot.

The respondent continued,

R03: Other people are going to read this somewhere, okay. [Maybe] they'll understand the impact this has. Maybe they'll be able to do something about it. It's only getting worse for [the administration] too. The more fights [the inmates] are having. The more people are trying to overdose in here. More people are trying to sneak stuff in. You know, they hate each other. They can't stand the staff. It's getting real bad. Imagine what's going to be like, you know, the closer it gets to the holidays, that's when it gets real bad for these guys. That's when a lot of the aggravation happens for them. This is a box this town put up just to put away people who were bad. They didn't care what happens to them.

It is evident that the jail experience had an effect on both the respondents and on the children who temporarily lost a father to the criminal justice system. Not surprisingly, many respondents expressed the belief that the impact of their incarceration on their paternal role would remain after their release.

POST-INCARCERATION PLANS AND EXPECTATIONS

One of the final questions that this project sought to address was, "what are the jailed fathers' plans and expectations regarding their paternal role following release?" As a group, the inmates who resided with children prior to incarceration (parents and "mixed" parents) had more realistic expectations regarding their post-incarceration roles than did the inmates who resided away from their children (biological fathers).

Nearly 92% (n = 11) of the inmates who resided with their children prior to incarceration planned to resume their paternal role after release. Seven of the 11 men voiced awareness of and concern about the amount of work they would need to do to re-establish relationships with their children. The first respondent spoke about having to work to rebuild his relationship with his son.

> IER: When you are released, where do you plan to live? Back in the same house?

> U36: Yes

> IER: What do you think will be the same and what will be different in your relationship with [son]?

> U36: [Son] is going to be older. So I'm going to have to, it's going to have to be, he's going to be changed. He's going to be a year older. At the age of 8, 9, and 10, one year is a big difference. I know that. Just from all of my brothers and sisters and my nieces and nephews. That's going to be...I have to leave that open. I can't expect to pick up where we left off. It's got to be new. I have to leave that open. If anything is the same, and I'm sure it will be, the first thing I know he's going to do is hug me. He's going to come running and give me a hug. Everything is not going to be perfect. I know that but I'm going to make it as best as I can, as good as possible. We'll work...things, they're going to be good.

The next respondent also spoke of the work he had ahead, when reunited with his wife and five children. He expressed fear that his youngest children would forget who he was, or be afraid of him.

> IER: Okay. When you leave here are you going to be living back at home with them?

> R05: Oh yeah.

IER: What do you think will be the same when you are released?

R05: Nothin. I'm going to have to work at returning to my children's lives. I'm going to have to work at returning to my marriage. Six months when you are out on the street, when you're out amongst people, amongst your family, is nothing. But if you've ever been away from your family for any period of time, one month is enough. One month is enough. Um... taking a trip and being away for one night, to me, is enough. The relationship that I share with my wife and children is one of a daily routine. We sit down and watch TV together in the evening. We eat dinner together. There are just certain things that we have always done together as a family. I was taken away from that and it hurts me and it hurts my wife and children.

IER: What do you think your relationship will be like with your children when you are released? How do you think they will act?

R05: I think because I've been away for so long, my oldest son is going to want to wrestle. And my five-year old daughter, she's daddy's girl, she...she's not only daddy's girl, but she's daddy shadow too. Every place I go, she is there. I would imagine things are going to be more emotional when I come home with her. She's going to cry and say, "Oh daddy I'm so happy your home." You know. "I missed you". And the other three I think honestly think they are probably going to shy away. [The twins], they're a year and a half old but I was in their lives the first year of their life and for a child, I would imagine, it's probably going to be pretty hard for them to remember me. Now they see me from time to time, they see me through this piece of glass. But, for a child, that's not enough. And I can say that, I'm not a psychologist, and I'm not, you know, an advocate, a child advocate but I can say that because I'm the man in the booth. Looking at them in the glass. I know. I'm the one that absorbs. I'm the one that stands here and watches their actions. I'm the one that watches when they get up and pound on the glass thing. They put their arms out like they want me to hold them. But I think when I finally do get out and I'm able to pick them up, I think that they'll probably end up shying away from me. And the same goes for my three-year old son. He knows me and I'm in his life and I've been with him all his life. But I think that he is just too young and the way that he's been talking to me, you know, "why don't you love us?" "Why don't you come home?" He thinks that this is my fault. He thinks that I want to be away. And I think that he's going to reject me whenever I get out. I honestly do. It's going to hurt if he does, but I'm prepared for it, you know. Because I'm thinking this way and I'm preparing myself for it. You know. So, it's going to be hard and I'm just going to have to work on it. There's...if something were done prior to me coming to jail or early on when I was in here, this could have been prevented. But, now, it's done. The damage is there. I'm just going to have to work on it. I'm going to have to do what I can to correct it.

Another respondent worried about resuming his relationship with his wife and daughter, while being "clean" from drugs for the first time in many years.

IER: When you leave here in a couple weeks, where are you going to be living?

U79: Back home.

IER: With [wife] and [daughter]?

U79: Yeah.

IER: What do you think that will be like?

U79: As far as you mean relationship or family? I think I'll go back to the way used to be. I know what it's like from a drug addict's point of view, and learning to live life clean is going to be different. I know...I'm expecting it to be tough. We're going away as soon as I get out. Within the first two days we're going somewhere. We're either going to Florida or we're going to Canada for like a week. I'm expecting to feel anxious. I'm expecting to feel angry and miserable because I'm going to be doing things clean that I never done before that I'm only used to doing on drugs whether [daughter] was there or not. When we were on the vacations I told you about when she was younger, I hid it pretty much, I thought I was anyway. They didn't know about it. But I was still doing things and enjoying DisneyWorld but I was high. It's going to be hard to go out and do it without being on something. It's going to be hard to learn to adapt to that. I think I'm going to be miserable.

IER: What do you think your relationship with [daughter] will be like when you go home?

U79: Hopefully...I know it's not going to be where we left off. Naturally it's going to be down. I'm going to make it strong and thoughtful. Do what I can to make sure...she knows that I love her. She knows I'll be there for her. But she also knows that physically I'm not there for her right now. There's a lot of things that she's gone through in the last two years that I just couldn't deal with because I wasn't able to. I think she's starting to rely on other people because naturally she has to rely on somebody. So I'm going to try to build that back up too.

Four of the respondents who resided with their children prior to their incarceration had less realistic expectations regarding the nature of their relationship with their children following their release. These four respondents believed that their children would harbor no ill feelings toward them and that their relationships would not be influenced by their incarceration. The following respondent illustrates this belief.

IER: Whenever you leave here where do you plan to live? With whom?

U39: I plan on living with my wife and children.

IER: What do you think will be the same?

U39: What do I think will be the same? I think the closeness that we all had before I came, you know. And the fun. The fun and the closeness.

IER: Okay. What will be different?

U39: Hmm. What will be different? (chuckles)   That's a tough one. There's got to be a lot that…Basically what will be different is me. I don't expect them to change all that much. I don't know. I think, it's hard. What will be different? I don't know. I don't know what will be different this time. I just don't know.

IER: What do you think your relationship with your kids will be like when you are released? How do you think they will react, first of all to you coming home?

U39: They'll be overjoyed I'm sure, just as I will be. You know, they'll be glad to have me home. I think…I don't know. It'll be just like one of those really…it'll be like a hallmark moment I guess. It'll just be, I don't know, it's hard to describe what I think it will be like. It's a tough question.

IER: Are you expecting a smooth transition?

U39: Yeah. Yeah, I'm not expecting…well, see I was sentenced to a program. So I have to go to a program, so I'll be on work release. I'll only be able to go, I'll be able to go home on weekends and everything. So that's pretty much preset, you know, the smooth transition back into family life and mainstream society. So…that's pretty much been prescribed for me.

The next respondent also indicated his belief that things would be "back to normal" after his incarceration. This belief was rooted in the fact that he and his daughters had endured much together, and he viewed his incarceration as one more thing they would get through.

> IER: What will your relationship with your daughters will be like when you leave?

> R11: It would go back to being the same. They are strong girls. They're very strong. They are. They are very, very strong. They hold their head high in a lot of things, they really do. Cause like I said, we've been through a lot. We have. We've really been through a lot. When you lose your home because you just ain't got no money, I mean that's a lot. They've held their head up, they really have. I hope and pray to God that it goes back to the same, which I do believe it will.

The majority of the inmates who resided with children prior to incarceration and planned to resume a paternal role following release were cognizant of the impact that their incarceration had on their relationships with their children. They were expecting their children to express anger, fear, or mistrust toward them and were anticipating that the re-establishment of a meaningful relationship to take time and effort.

Biological Parents

The expectations of the inmates who resided apart from their children stand in contrast to those highlighted above. Three of the 12 respondents had little to no contact with their children prior to incarceration and reported no plans to increase their paternal role upon release. The first respondent saw his children approximately once every two weeks prior to his incarceration. He reported that he planned to reside with his girlfriend after release. The interviewer asked about his relationship with his three children.

> IER: Do you plan to live in the same area that they (children) live?

U03: Oh no. They live in [names town]. I live in [names town].

IER: So a little bit of distance. What do you think will be the same when you are released and what do you think will be different?

U03: I know their appearance will be different. I know their appearance when I get out and actually touch them is going to be a lot of different. Kicking with them. Since I've been in here I know that the issues that we've talked about since I've been in here, we'll be able to talk a lot more freely. Especially since they are a year older, each one of them. They know how to talk to me a little bit better now. They've learned just as well as I have from this. Just as much as me they learned. I know that they got a lot of questions. Lot more than what they had before. I know that they can't wait to shoot them at me. Test me on some things. I know that they're going to be a lot more not spying but I know they're going to be a lot of checking up on me.

IER: Do you think they're going to be skeptical?

U03: Yeah. That's the word. It'll be a lot skeptical. But in the same sense, they are going to be praying and hoping that I don't have to go through this any more.

IER: What do you think your relationship with your kids will be like when you're released? You mentioned that [son] is angry

U03: Yeah, well he'll get over it. I'll have to work on that with him. You can't answer that as far as my relationship, as far as my love for him, it will never change. Regardless what situation they put me in. They put me in a prison cell away for a year. It wouldn't change that. Nothing. I think my relationship with my children should be a lot stronger.

IER: How do you think they are going to react to you coming home?

U03: Oh they're going to be happy, yeah. They're going to be very happy. I know they're not going to want to go nowhere for a while. They're going to probably come...I know especially [youngest son]. He's going to want to come stay over there on the weekends and things like that.

Nine respondents planned to resume their paternal role, but only two respondents articulated realistic plans for doing so. These two respondents recognized that they had limited contact with their children prior to their incarceration, and that their children may not want contact with them following their release. Both of these inmates had children who were teenaged or older, and they articulated that their children would help determine the extent of the relationships. The following respondent expressed his concern that his son may not be ready or willing to re-establish a relationship with his father.

IER: When you are released, where do you plan on living?

U38: I don't know. I'm going to talk to my lawyer. I want to get sentenced to a halfway house drug program. If I have to go somewhere I'd like to put my life back on track. I know that I don't want to go look for my old lady, my girlfriend that I was living with cause I know where that road would just lead again. I want to straighten my life out. I want to have a relationship with my son and my family and stuff again. I miss them. They tell me they love me but they don't know what to do with me (chuckles). They say they are waiting for the phone call when I call them up and say, "hey, I don't need nothing. Just calling to see how everybody is." I'd like to make that phone call.

IER: What do you think will be the same in your relationship with [son]?

U38: I'd like to go back to being his friend. That's what I want to be the same. I want to be my kid's friend again. I want to be close to him. I want him to come and talk to me about things again. Listen to what wisdom I do have from this stupid life that I led.

IER: And what do you think is going to be different?

U38: I don't know. I'm kind of scared that maybe it's all going to be different. Maybe this time he's not going to let me waltz back in and just be his friend again. Maybe he is going to tired of this time and say, "hey, dad." That's the part that scares me. Not much has changed again.

Two respondents indicated that they planned to first get their drug addiction under control, and then move back with their families. Both of these respondents reported they had abandoned their families as a result of their drug addiction. Further, both respondents indicated a desire to go to an in-patient program upon release from the jail. These respondents articulated "a plan" to tackle their addiction, but had no "plan" for rekindling the relationship with their children. They seemed to believe that, once they had completed their "program," they would simply walk back into their children's lives and pick up where they left off, with no hard feelings.

IER: When you are released, where do you plan to live and with whom?

U23: Well, again, let me just tell you, when I leave, I requested to go to an in-patient program. Because by no means am I recovered. I will never be well. I'll be an addict the rest of my life. I'm not ready and I'm not going to kid myself. This is the first time that I've ever even remotely thought of this. Even going into a program. This is the first program that I've ever been in. I want to suck up all the knowledge it is that I can suck up and I'm not going to short myself of any of it. I'm not going to fool myself because I don't want to take any chances. This is my life, this is my livelihood. Without my life it can't work. I can't love anyone. The person that I was, I don't like. The person that I've seen, I don't like that person when I'm on drugs.

IER: You mentioned that you are hoping to go back with your family?

U23: Definitely.

IER: Okay. Whenever you are home again, what do you think will be the same and what will be different?

U23: What's going to be the same is the attention that I show [daughter]. What will be different? I'm going to focus more on what will be different because I was lacking something from the start, which was a spiritual foundation. This is what will be different.

IER: What do you think your relationship is going to be like with [daughter]?

U23: I think it's going to be beautiful. Very beautiful. It can't be nothing but beautiful. I mean she still respects me. I haven't lost that. I'm quite sure of that. I'll spend more time with her now.

IER: How do you think she is going to react?

U23: Well, who knows? Kids are funny. I can only reflect on how it was and we never parted on bad terms. And the fact that when I parted the genuine hurt and concern that she felt for me I would think that by me coming back would be a blessing. When you get attached to someone like that it's not like, "okay you left, stay away, stay away. Kids are not like that. I've never shown her anything but positive, anything but good. Other than the fact that I was abusing drugs around her.

The final five nonresidential respondents reported that not only did they plan to "be a father" again, they planned to increase their paternal role with their children. These individuals foresaw a future where they lived with their children (in one case, all 3 children from three different relationships), and supported them emotionally (e.g. "being there for them," doing homework, playing, etc.), and financially. These respondents articulated a future that was in no way linked to their past behavior. Their descriptions sounded more like a wish or a dream, rather than a realistic outcome.

The first respondent had been jailed for approximately one year. He has three daughters by three different women. Upon release he planned to live with his fiancée and their 14-month-old daughter.

IER: After your release, are you planning to live back with [daughter] and your fiancée?

U29: Yes.

IER: What do you think it's going to be like?

U29: The same except...everything will be the same except me. I'm not going to get back out. I've got some things together here. I ain't going back out there hustling. I'm not going back out. I'm going to get me a good job to take care of them while I go to school. It's going to be hard going to school at night and working. I ain't used to doing nothing. Since I was like 11, 12 years old I've been hustling things. I was making my money fast and easy. So I ain't never worked for real. I think things are going to be basically the same. Once I get there, be there for about a week or so. She'll [youngest daughter] realize that I'm going to be there. She'll realize that I'm a part of her life. Like I said, I'm going to get [4-year-old daughter] over living with us too. I'm going to send her to school and bring her up. It's going to be the opposite of the way it's been. Like she was living with her mom but coming to stay with me for a couple weeks, a month or so. But now she's going to be staying with me and going to see her mom like that. Like weekends and when she ain't in school or whatever. Things going to be good. Things are going to work out. I get back closer to [other 4-year-old daughter]. I basically know how that's going to happen too. Once I get her back other there with us and she gets with her sisters and start playing, she'll get used to being around, she get used to being around me again. Get used to seeing me there because, like I said, it's going to be different if I ain't going to be in and out all the time. Except when I'm at work or at school or whatever but other than that, I'm going to be there. I'll always be there.

IER: How do you think your daughters will react when they first see you?

U29: [4-year-old] is going to be shy. She ain't going to really know how to come at me. I think [other 4-year-ol] is going to come right up and hug me. [Youngest daughter], she's so young, she's friendly with everyone. My girl said she won't go to no dudes, none of her cousins, granddad, uncles, she won't go to no dudes. For some reason, when she see me I think she going to come right to me. Hold her arms out and come right to me, I think she is. I think [older daughter] is going to run right up and hug me too.

IER: Do you think any of your children will have any negative reactions?

U29: I don't know. I hope not. Like I said, I think I'm pretty good with those two. [Older daughter], I'm going to have to build that back up. Get her know me, get her to like me again. Candy, (chuckles) you know what I'm saying. Things like that. She'll come around. She'll see how the other girls react to me. She'll realize that she's the same as them. She's my daughter just like they are. And she should be reacting to me the same way. So I think things are going to work out. I'm going to have all three of them together a lot when I get out too. Make sure they grow up together, know each other, be close to each other.

The next respondent has four children by four different women. He has never lived with any of his children or with their mothers. Still, this individual envisioned playing a much more important role in their lives upon release.

IER: How do you deal with being apart from your kids?

U93: How? I mean how could...what other way can you deal with it? When you ain't accustomed to missing nothing. That's what it is. I mean you think about it.

IER: If I understand what your saying, you don't know if your missing something because your not...

U93: You're not a part of it.

IER: When you are released, what do you think will be different and what do you think will be the same?

U93: What will be different is that I'm looking forward to is this program. I'm not saying that this program is everything but it would be a major part in my stepping out there because the [program]is a place where you can get started like a re-entry program back in the society. So I want to use that to the best of my ability where it will tie me in with my children. I got a chance to use this program to get myself an apartment and keep steady work. So once I complete that then I can have my children come over and spend the night. My family can come visit me. That's what I'm looking forward to. I'm looking forward to just being a whole 360 degree turn around. That's what I'm looking for.

IER: What do you think your relationship will be like with your children?

U93: Beautiful. I can't keep them off me. You know they'll be so affectionate. "Why can't I stay over here tonight."

"Because your mother needs you." I know my children will be so affectionate that they won't be able to keep their hands off me. Lots of hugs and kisses. I already seen it before. You know how Bill Cosby was with his family? I don't to see myself exactly like him but I see myself wise enough to take some of that from him and pass it on to my children. The humor and understanding. So that's the relationship that I see with my children. Being real affectionate with me.

There was great disjuncture between the nature of the father-child relationships prior to incarceration and the ones that these five fathers envisioned after release. Their words sounded hollow and insincere and belied their actions. They failed to articulate awareness that their children may be hesitant to interact with them. The post-incarceration plans of the biological fathers, as a group, seemed to capture their lack of connectedness with their children.

SUMMARY

The data from the current study indicates that the jail experience of fathers who resided with their children prior to incarceration is different from the experience of fathers who did not reside with their children prior to their incarceration.

The fathers who resided apart from their children prior to incarceration were less likely to maintain contact with their children while jailed, but were generally satisfied with the visits when they occurred. They were less likely to report that their incarceration had negatively affected their children's emotional or financial well-being. Remarkably, one-half of the interviewees who resided apart from their children believed that their incarceration had a positive impact on their children.

In contrast, the fathers who resided with their children prior to their incarceration experienced anguish as a result of their separation from children. These fathers either refused to permit their children to visit at the jail, and/or had negative experiences when their children did visit. This group of fathers was also more likely to report that their children were "worse off" emotionally and financially as a result of their incarceration. The lack of contact with their children resulted in greater frequencies of loneliness for the men who previously resided with their children. These "parents" expressed concern of the lasting effects of their incarceration on their relationships with their children. The "pains of imprisonment" (Sykes, 1958) promise to reach beyond the walls for these fathers as they attempt to re-establish relationships with their children.

CHAPTER 6

Conclusions and Implications

As a nation, we continue to incarcerate individuals at an astonishing rate. The most recent statistics indicate that our jails are home to 592,462 persons, of whom 89% are men (Gilliard, 1999). As the rate of incarceration has continued to increase, so too has the magnitude of enforced separation from children. Consequently, more and more children experience the episodic absence of their fathers due to our correctional policies.

Data from the current study confirm that the paternal role is an important one for the inmate fathers and it is one that a sizeable proportion takes seriously. The data further confirm that incarceration is painful for the inmate fathers who had formed attachments with their children.

The purpose of this chapter is to discuss the implications of this study and to make recommendations for addressing the problems facing jailed fathers and their children. The chapter focuses on four broad areas. First, a reexamination of the research questions and discussion of the data generated is presented. Second, the linkages between the findings and the theoretical framework of attachment theory are discussed. Next, the discussion focuses on policy and methodological implications derived from this study. The chapter concludes with suggestions for future research and an overview of the limitations of this study.

RESEARCH QUESTIONS AND ASSOCIATED FINDINGS

The research questions are presented below, with a brief discussion of the findings highlighted previously in Chapters 4 – 6.

What are the Family Characteristics of the Inmate Fathers' Families of Origin?

Nearly one-half of the jailed fathers reported that both parents were involved in their upbringing.   An additional one-third of the respondents were reared by their mother only. As highlighted earlier, children reared in single-mother homes face greater hardships, both in childhood and in later life, than do their counterparts reared in two-parent families. These hardships include lower family incomes during childhood, higher rates of school dropout, and lower earning potential in adulthood (Wilson, 1996).

Approximately 20% of the interview respondents had parents who had been incarcerated. In the majority of cases, the parent was the father. Additionally, 36% of interview respondents had an immediate family member (sibling, child) who had been incarcerated.   The interview data clearly indicate that many of the interview respondents (56%) have experienced losing a loved one to incarceration.

How were the Inmate Fathers Parented during Childhood?

An important outcome of the present study was the development of the Paternal Typology that was derived from the interview data. This typology was used to categorize the childhood experiences and interactions between the jailed fathers and their own fathers. The large majority of interview respondents (64%) had negative experiences in their relationship with their fathers. The most common paternal type was the "Absent" father, experienced by 40% percent of the interviewees (n=10). Twelve percent of interview respondents had "Abusive" fathers, 12% of these respondents had "Addicted" fathers, and 16% of the interview respondents had "Workaholic" fathers. Thus,

64% of the interview respondents had negative paternal models. Only 20% of the interview respondents had fathers that were "Loving and Supportive."

What are the Characteristics of the Pre-Incarceration Relationships between Jailed Fathers and their Children?

The respondents in the current study had an average of 2.0 minor children, with an average age of 7.32 years. Five respondents in the current study had adult children only, and four respondents reported that their child had been born during their incarceration. Thus, 89% of the respondents (n = 83) had minor children prior to their incarceration. Among these respondents, the majority (n = 46, 55%) was not residing with any of their minor children in the six months prior to incarceration. Among respondents who were residing with minor children, 17 fathers were living with all of their minor children, and 20 fathers were residing with only some of their minor children.

Both survey and interview data indicate the fathers' beliefs that they, along with mothers, play a critical role in the lives of their children. Despite these beliefs, the men who resided apart from their children had infrequent contact with them, which diminishes the positive influence a father can exert. As reported in Chapter V, many of the interview respondents who did not live with their children were themselves reared in father-absent homes and were ill prepared for the birth of their child and the amount of time and energy required of parents. Drug addiction was an additional impediment to successful fulfillment of the paternal role for some of these fathers. Erosion of the father-child relationship was common and severe for drug-addicted fathers. Unfortunately, it is not until they are "clean," which often occurs inside the correctional institution, that they recognize the impact of their behavior on their children. Also, given the rate at which addicts return to their drug use, it is not a forgone conclusion that these revelations will yield any significant changes in the father-child relationship.

Conversely, the respondents who resided with some or all of their children prior to their incarceration spent much more time interacting with their children. The interview accounts indicate that these fathers were involved in the lives of their children. They provided detailed descriptions of the activities that they shared, and of their children's personalities. It is evident that the paternal role was integral for these respondents.

What is the Nature and Significance of Contact with Family During Incarceration?

The respondents in the current study had limited face-to-face contact with their minor children during incarceration. Approximately 48% of respondents reported visiting with their minor children during incarceration and approximately 68% had spoken to their children by telephone.

A significant finding relates to differing views between Parents and Biological fathers about visitation. The interview data revealed that the men who had resided with children pre-incarceration were much more likely to refuse visits with their children than were men who had not resided with their children. The reasons for refusing contact with children included the emotional distress for both fathers and children that accompanies seeing loved ones through a pane of glass, and other environmental conditions present in the jail (e.g. lack of privacy, visitation policies and practices). These respondents identified both emotional and behavioral changes in their children as a result of their incarceration. Additionally, the men who had resided with their children were much less satisfied with their visits than were the men who had resided apart from their children.

In stark contrast, the interview respondents who had not resided with their children prior to incarceration spoke favorably of their face-to-face visits with their children. The interview data clearly indicate that the focus was on the benefits for the respondents, and not their children. One-half of these respondents believed that their incarceration had positive effects on their children, including increased contact and communication, and providing an example for their children of what occurs to individuals who break the law. The positive view that these respondents had of the contact with their children is depressing. It suggests that these fathers were out of "sync" with their children, which is not surprising given the lack of contact and absence of emotional connection that characterized the relationships between these respondents and their children.

In addition to face-to-face contact, the respondents reported on telephone contact with loved ones. The important, and consistent, message that was delivered from all of the respondents was that telephone contact was very expensive. As a result of the costs associated with making telephone calls, this type of contact was unavailable for many inmates. As Creasie Finney-Hairston (1998) has stated,

"The collect-call telephone policies that have made prison telephones a lucrative business for prisons and telephone companies also affect the fathers' relationships with their children. At first glance, telephone contact seems like a good way to maintain relationships. Prison talk, however, is not cheap" (p. 626).

For inmates whose family members could not afford, or accept, collect calls, telephone contact is not an option.

Do the Pre-Incarceration Relationships of Jailed Fathers Impact the Stress of Incarceration?

The pre-incarceration relationships of the jailed fathers did impact the stress of incarceration in the current study. Respondents who resided with some or all of their children prior to incarceration reported higher frequencies of loneliness than did the respondents who lived apart from their children.

The greater frequencies of loneliness reported by fathers who resided with their children prior to incarceration, while not surprising, is important. As Fromm-Reichman (1976) suggests, "loneliness in its own right plays a much more significant role in the dynamics of mental disturbances than we have so far been ready to acknowledge" (cited in Rokach, 1998, p. 4). According to Rokach (1998), while there is overlap between loneliness and depression, they are qualitatively different affective responses.

"Usually when we are lonely we yearn for the company and caring of others; that is we want to reach out and connect with a support network, friends, or loved ones. Depression, on the other hand, elicits the opposite reaction. When depressed, most people seem to prefer to be left alone to attend to their pain. They withdraw into themselves by cutting themselves off from the rest of the world" (p. 4).

The interview data confirm that the jailed fathers who resided with their children prior to incarceration missed their children deeply. They expressed sorrow, disappointment in themselves, and hopelessness over being separated from their children. It seems reasonable that interventions aimed at increased quality contact between jailed fathers and loved ones (especially children), would be met favorably by these respondents, and could be successful at reducing feelings of loneliness among fathers who had significant father-child relationships prior to their incarceration. However, interventions aimed at increasing contact must be able to accommodate the concerns the jailed fathers expressed about bringing their children into the jail environment.

What are the Jailed Fathers' Plans and Expectations regarding their Paternal Role Following Release?

A large majority (21 of 25, 84%) of the jailed fathers interviewed anticipated resuming their paternal role upon release. However, the jailed fathers who had resided with their children prior to incarceration had much more realistic expectations regarding the re-establishment of the father-child relationship, than did the fathers who resided apart from their children prior to incarceration. The "parents" and "mixed parents" voiced awareness of the impact that their jail term had on their relationships. These fathers were anxious about their post-incarceration relationships with their children, and some expressed fear that their children will be resistant to interactions with them, or will have forgotten them completely.

Conversely, the non-resident fathers were less concerned about being rebuffed by their children following release, and many of these individuals anticipated an expanded paternal role and a more significant father-child relationship than existed prior to their incarceration. Once again, the interview data suggest that the respondents who lived apart from their children, and had very limited contact with them, were not "attuned" to their children. These respondents failed to view the "father-child" relationship as one that is complex, and that develops over years of both joyful and demanding interactions. Most distressing of all is that the absence of attachment between father and child is a predictable outcome given the childhood experiences of these men, and may lead to a continuation of the cycle of absent fathers.

LINKAGES BETWEEN FINDINGS AND ATTACHMENT THEORY

The task at this stage is to be able to simultaneously view the respondents as both children and parents. To do so is to begin to understand how events that occurred 15-20 years ago (as children) can influence behavior today (as parents). To do so is to see the jailed fathers as both a "by-product" of their experiences, and as a "manufacturer" of similar experiences for their children. Attachment theory provides the framework for the exploration of these linkages.

Attachment theory suggests that a bonding process occurs between parent and child and, from this relationship, important lessons and behaviors are learned by both. Adult parents' childhood experiences, particularly the parenting they experienced and the attachments they formed or failed to form, play a significant role in their subsequent parenting. "There is strong evidence that how attachment behaviour comes to be organized within an individual turns in high degree on the kinds of experience he has in his family of origin, or, if he is unlucky, out of it" (Bowlby, 1988, p. 4).

While early attachment researchers focused almost exclusively on mother-child attachment, evidence now suggests that both mother-child and father-child attachments are important to the development of the child (Lamb, 1981; Yogman, et al, 1988; Bronstein, 1988; Main and Weston, 1981). In fact, according to Dr. Robert Moradi, "children whose fathers help care for them are less likely to become violent, they have higher IQ's, better impulse control, better social adaptations" (as cited in Adler, 1997, p.73).

The most important suggestion from attachment theory, for the present study, is that individuals learn how to be a parent from their own parents (Bowlby, 1952; 1988).

"There is, of course, much clinical evidence that a mother's feeling for and behaviour toward her baby are deeply influenced also by her previous personal experiences, especially those she has had and may still be having with her own parents; and though the evidence of this in regard to the father's attitudes is less plentiful, what there is clearly points to the same conclusion" (Bowlby, 1988, p. 15).

As reported earlier, a majority of the interview respondents had either negative interactions with, or little to no contact with their fathers. Forty percent of the interview respondents grew up absent the guiding hand of their own father and 20% reported that their father was abusive. Additionally, 20% of the interview respondents reported that a parent had been incarcerated. The extent of family disturbance, especially the father-child bond, was great for the interview respondents as children.

The current study lends support to attachment theory, particularly with regard to those respondents who had "Absent" fathers (n = 10). The reasons for paternal absence included parental separation and divorce (n=5), military duty and other work obligations (n = 3), abandonment (n = 1) and paternal incarceration (n = 1). Importantly, the reasons for paternal absence did not seem to moderate the effect of being reared without a father. Of the 10 interview respondents who had "Absent" fathers as children, 8 of these respondents were "Absent" fathers themselves. The other two respondents resided with all or some of their children. Interestingly, one of the latter individuals was reared by his grandmother (hence, both mother and father were "absent" from his life, for the most part). He described his grandmother as a warm and loving "parent," and because of her age, she did not work which permitted the respondent to spend a great deal of time with her. Thus, while he had "absent" biological parents, he was reared in an environment with a wonderful parental model.

Another example of "modeling" came from the respondents with "Abusive" fathers. The author was surprised that all three respondents who experienced abuse as children stated that they had learned "what not to do" from their fathers. Their reports indicate that in some instances they sought out other models (grandparents or parents of their friends) and "watched" their parental behavior. Further, while the most salient paternal characteristic recalled by these respondents was their fathers' abusiveness, it was not the only characteristic recalled. Two of the three respondents reported positive aspects of their fathers' behavior (e.g. going to work, going on outings). Consequently, because their fathers were present, these respondents observed him in situations in which he was not abusive. Further, as the respondents became parents themselves, their perspectives of their fathers moderated, and two of the three respondents implied they had forgiven their dads. This permitted them to "adopt" the positive behaviors modeled by their fathers, while working on avoiding the problematic behaviors. This same opportunity was not afforded the men whose fathers were absent.

One of the interesting findings regarding the group of "absent" fathers was the disjuncture between their beliefs about the behavior of a "good" father and the significance of his role, and their actions in fulfilling this role. The interview respondents who were "Absent" fathers could clearly articulate what good fathers do for their children, yet they were not living up to their own standards. Leon Pitts, Jr. (1999) describes men who grew up with no father as having "missing pieces" (pp. 19-20) that affect them in adulthood. As he explains, men who had absent fathers,

> "Didn't have that someone who teaches you 'man' things and makes you want so badly to learn, so desperately to please him – as if his approving nod might validate your entire life. Didn't have that man who makes things right by the force of his presence, like having [Michael] Jordan on your team in the last minutes of a crucial game" (Pitts, Jr., 1999, p. 20).

According to John Bowlby (1988), parents who have had disturbed childhoods (e.g. separation from their own parents) tend to engage in less frequent interaction with their own children than do parents with happier childhoods. It appears as if the respondents who grew up without the active presence of their fathers may be doing the best job they can, absent paternal role models. An unfortunate outcome, though, is that the children of these respondents are experiencing their childhood with an absent father. Therefore, it is critical to recognize the opportunity that incarceration affords to influence the future paternal behavior of these jailed fathers, and the potential for effecting improvement in the lives of their children. An opportunity exists to weaken or break a cycle that, without intervention, seems destined to a downward spiral.

John Bowlby (1988) suggests that all human beings have, at birth, a wide array of "pathways" along which to develop. "Which particular pathway he proceeds along is determined by the environment he meets with, especially the way his parents (or parent substitutes) treat him, and how he responds to them" (Bowlby, 1988, p. 136). Responsive and "attuned" parents create a climate that permits development along healthy pathways. Conversely, "those who have insensitive, unresponsive, neglectful, or rejecting parents are likely to develop along a deviant pathway" (Bowlby, 1988, p. 136). Involvement in criminal activity, arrests, and incarceration, would have to be considered an unhealthy or "deviant" pathway.

The perspective of simultaneously viewing the jailed fathers as "children" and "parents" is critical for several reasons. First, it enhances our understanding of the influence of childhood experiences and the role they play in an individual's development along "deviant" pathways. Second, it forces recognition that our correctional policies have ripple effects that impact the children of those incarcerated, and in turn, their children, and so on. For, while approximately one-half of jailed fathers resided apart from their children prior to incarceration, for the fathers who resided with their children and for whom the paternal role was integral, incarceration very effectively severs the father-child ties. Thus, these men are now "absent" from their children's lives. We must, as a society, recognize the paternal status of our inmates, for the failure to do so will inevitably result in the repetition of this pattern.

While it is not possible to reverse the hands of time and alter the childhood experiences of the jailed fathers, it is not too late to provide alternative information to temper what they have learned from their experiences. As John Bowlby (1988) argues,

"Although the capacity for developmental change diminishes with age, change continues throughout the life cycle so that changes for better or worse are always possible. It is this continuing potential for change that means at no time of life is a person invulnerable to every possible adversity and also that at no time of life is a person impermeable to favourable influence" (p. 136).

One positive impact of incarceration may be that it gives an individual an opportunity to "take stock" of his life. Most individuals reflect on their situations and "an emotional inventory is taken in which a man assesses his assets and liabilities and makes an estimate of his worth to himself and others" (Gibbs, 1982, p. 102). Many of the jailed fathers in the current study concluded that there was room for improvement in their relationships with their children. Thus, when men are jailed a unique opportunity exists to attempt intervention at a time when many men are receptive. Interventions must recognize the parental status of incarcerated men, and their unique histories, if change is to be effected.

In the current study, nearly 78% (n = 72) of the respondents indicated interest in participating in parenting programs during their incarceration. It is possible that this interest reflects more the inmates' desires to be occupied, rather than a strong desire to improve their parenting. On the other hand, it could reflect the outcome of the respondents' emotional inventories. Regardless of the motivation, the opportunity exists to provide information on and instruction in parenting to individuals who are amenable to obtaining this information.

POLICY AND PROGRAMMATIC IMPLICATIONS

The present study is an exploratory and descriptive effort aimed at increased understanding of an extremely understudied population – jailed fathers. It is beyond the scope of this project to make broad and sweeping generalizations, but the findings make it is possible to delineate two major multi-faceted policy considerations, aimed at these forgotten parents. The first relates to the identification and description of jailed fathers. The second relates to maintenance of family bonds between jailed fathers and their children.

Identification and Description of Inmate Fathers

When an individual is convicted of a crime, punishment is a frequent consequence. Punishing the "individual" convicted, however, is a legal fiction as it is obvious that the loved ones of the convicted individual are punished as well. It is certainly not debatable that our correctional policies generally overlook this reality. This observation is supported by the simple fact that there are no national statistics on the number of children affected by parental incarceration, especially with regard to incarcerated fathers. This lack of data is significant, for it reflects our myopic view of male inmates, whereby we strip them of all family roles. It is much "easier" to incarcerate a "criminal" when they are not viewed as sons, brothers, husbands, and perhaps most specifically, as fathers. This also reflects our arrogance and ignorance in believing that incarcerated fathers lack the capacity to be good fathers. This results in a shortsighted approach that negates our (purported) efforts to curb the cycle of crime and incarceration. Thus, it is imperative that we: (1) recognize the parental status of incarcerated fathers, and (2) systematically gather information on the number of men who are fathers and the number of minor children they have.

The current study presents an image of inmates that is in stark contrast to the stereotype that has become a part of our social perceptions. As would any cross-section from our society, the respondents in the current study encompassed a broad continuum of paternal behavior. The study sample included both "deadbeat" dads, who had difficulty remembering the ages of their children, and "involved and loving" fathers, who were the primary caregivers prior to their incarceration. Prior studies have failed to recognize these differences, lumping all male respondents into one of two categories: "father" (has children), or "not a father" (has no children). This study clearly identified the differences between the fathers who were "attuned" to their children, and those who were not, and there were significant differences.

It is clear that the needs and concerns of "parents" differ from those of "biological fathers." Hence it is necessary to delineate the level of involvement that existed between father and child prior to incarceration. It is this author's contention that if resources do not permit large scale programming, the men who were involved in the lives of children prior to incarceration should receive special consideration as participants.

Maintenance of Family Bonds

The respondents in the current study complained that the costs associated with telephone communication were prohibitive to maintaining contact. In addition, the unpleasant atmosphere that exists for both family members (Sturges, 1999) and for inmates during face-to-face visits made this form of family contact unappealing for many of the jailed fathers in the current study. Being forced to view loved one's through a piece of glass was more than most "attuned" fathers could bear. Consequently, communication and interactions between father and child are severely restricted during incarceration. Creasie Finney-Hairston (1998) argues, however, that the rules pertaining to contact between inmate and family "frequently bear little relevance to correctional goals and are insensitive to the family structures and needs" (p. 624). The lack of, or absence of, contact during incarceration makes reunification more difficult. A separation of six months can seem an eternity for young children. The interview respondents in the current study articulated their concerns that their children will have forgotten them, or will be resistant to interacting with them, upon release.

The administrators of correctional facilities must accommodate many competing goals. Obviously, facility security, staff and inmate safety, and punishment are central priorities (Cripe, 1997). At first glance, these goals appear to be in direct opposition with assisting inmates in maintaining contact and interaction with their children. Thus, in order to achieve the first set of goals, contact between inmates and their family members is highly regulated (Hairston, 1998). However, most fail to realize that programs designed to assist inmates in maintaining family relationships while incarcerated can assist administrators and staff members in achieving their primary goals of safety and security. Research has demonstrated that family maintenance programs can result in a decrease in discipline problems within the institution (Bayse, Algid, and Van Wyk, 1991), and they can improve an individual's successful release from incarceration (Carlson and Cervera, 1992).

Hence, a second policy implication relates to the critical need for father-child interaction during incarceration. It is imperative that jailed fathers be permitted to interact with their children in a more natural manner, and that jail administrators view this as a priority. There are ways to accommodate both safety and security issues (facility, staff, and inmate) and family maintenance issues. The first step is to recognize that "father-child interaction" is as critical to the effective operation of jails as the other organizational goals outlined above. This recognition would allow for the development of family-oriented policies and directives, and would encourage the exploration of existing programs that permit the simultaneous accomplishment of both "safety and security" and "family maintenance."

The following specific program recommendations are related to the policy implication outlined above. They were generated from (1) the current study and (2) a survey conducted by the Family and Corrections Network (FCN). The FCN surveyed thirty agencies that provide parenting programs in correctional facilities to identify key components of such programs (FCN report, 1995, issue 5, p. 6).

Evaluation and Needs Assessments of Jailed Fathers

The current study clearly identified that jailed fathers have various needs pertaining to their families. For example, many fathers desired to maintain contact with their children, but they did not want their children to be exposed to the jail environment. Many fathers complained about the costs associated with telephone contact. The point that must be re-emphasized is that jailed fathers, as a group, have needs that differ from other male inmates. Further, fathers who lived with their children prior to incarceration will have different needs than the fathers who lived apart from their children. Hence, the necessary first step of any successful family maintenance program is the assessment of needs of jailed fathers. The resulting program(s) should target the specific needs of the jailed fathers.

Children's Visiting Program

The jailed fathers in the current study expressed concern about subjecting their children to the jail environment. Specifically, the environmental conditions that were most problematic were: (1) noncontact visits occurred through a piece of glass, and (2) the visiting areas were either (a) cramped or (b) afforded no privacy. Thus, jails should provide a child-centered visiting area. This could be a relatively small space that is decorated appropriately for children, and contains materials conducive to positive interactions between fathers and their children (e.g. books, board games, art supplies, etc.).

Permitting fathers contact visits is imperative. However, contact visits could be a privilege, not a right, which the jailed fathers earn through participation in parenting classes and avoidance of disciplinary problems. There are model programs, many of them in female correctional facilities, which could be replicated in male facilities. One such program is "Project IMPACT" at SCI-Muncy, one of Pennsylvania's two prisons for women. This program utilizes a child-centered visiting room that resembles a daycare room for visits between mothers and their children. The benefits of these types of programs affect not only jailed fathers and their children, but also the correctional facilities.

Other Family Maintenance Programs

Not every incarcerated father will be able to engage in contact visits with their children while incarcerated. Therefore, it is critical that opportunities are afforded incarcerated fathers for maintaining contact with their loved ones in other ways. There are programs currently in place in some correctional facilities that encourage the maintenance of "long-distance" relationships. One approach permits incarcerated fathers to make either an audiotape or videotape while reading a children's book. These tapes are then sent home to their children. It seems reasonable that the reverse could happen, also, and children could make tapes for their fathers. While these interactions may not be as satisfying as contact visits, they do permit for communication between father and child.

Parent Education

As delineated in the current study, parenting is a learned skill. Parenting classes can provide information to assist jailed fathers in becoming more competent parents. There are numerous programs in place in correctional facilities across the country and it is beyond the scope of this discussion to detail these. However, many of the programs contain information on child development, communication, stress management, and discipline.

A recent study (Harrison, 1997) concluded that participation in parental training led to improved attitudes regarding child rearing among a group of incarcerated fathers. Parent education can be a way to effect positive change between parent and child both during incarceration and after release. Further, as we continue to expand our criminal justice policies, it seems critical that parent education programs target not only jailed fathers, but other populations as well (e.g. youthful offenders, and probation populations).

Community Based Support Services

Any effort to improve inmate-family relationships must recognize the critical period of reunification after release. However, most (if not all) correctional programs end when an inmate walks out the door of the jail. It seems critical that there is follow-up on parenting concerns and/or successes. As reported in Chapter 6, the jailed fathers reported both emotional and behavioral changes in their children. These behaviors and emotions are not going to disappear miraculously when the father reappears in his children's lives. It seems likely that the newly released father, in addition to readjusting to his freedom, will have to readjust to his children, as well. Even the best-intentioned (and competent) parents can wilt when children are demanding and disruptive.

The jailed fathers in the current study expressed concern and anxiety regarding their post-incarceration relationships with their children. Without a support system in place, their fears may come to fruition. Nearly 25 years ago, Jim Munro (1976) argued for an "open systems" view of criminal justice. Under this view there is recognition of the overlap between "criminal justice" and "social services." There is acknowledgement that distinct agencies (e.g. jails and social services) share common clients. Adoption of this perspective would require that jail administrators identify appropriate "parenting" services that exist in the community, and encourage jailed fathers to "hook into" these community-based support services prior to their release.

METHODOLOGICAL IMPLICATIONS

One of the strengths of this study was the utilization of a multi-method approach in examining the concerns of the jailed fathers. The questionnaire data was complemented and fleshed out by the interview based descriptions provided by the jailed fathers regarding their separation from their children. Still, the methods are not without limitations and these are discussed below.

Questionnaire

Data from both the pilot study (Hanrahan et al., 1996; Martin et al., 1995) and the current study clearly indicate that the issues associated with this topic and this population are very complex. The pilot study demonstrated that the sole use of questionnaires was not a viable strategy with this population for several reasons. First, literacy concerns limit the usefulness of questionnaires among incarcerated populations. Second, incarcerated individuals represent a group that, for the most part, is unaccustomed to completing "paper and pencil" forms. Finally, the complexity of the issues under examination (family characteristics, interactions with children) makes survey construction (especially the response categories) difficult. As outlined in Chapter 4, there were some validity issues related to some of the questionnaire items in the current study.

Data from the questionnaire highlight again that researchers should be aware of the limitations with using self-report surveys with incarcerated populations. As outlined in Chapter 3, to address literacy and other issues, the researcher used small-group administration of the questionnaire. However, many respondents chose to work at their own pace, which led to misinterpretation of items and response categories. The researcher believes that, when possible, questionnaires should be administered one-on-one to reduce the number of incorrect responses.

Face-to-Face Interviews

The second method employed was face-to-face interviews, which provided detailed and vivid accounts of the jailed fathers, their families of origin, and their experiences with their children (both prior to and during incarceration). The qualitative data allowed for fuller understanding of the quantitative data.

The researcher had experience and training in interviewing, and this seemed a necessity when eliciting emotional information from respondents. It is also suggests that researchers be aware of the potential for painful and traumatic accounts of childhood experiences with this population. It is imperative to be able to accept these accounts in an objective and non-judgmental manner. That is not to say that there is no effect – and it is essential, for both respondents and researchers, to have a way to "debrief" after explorations of this nature. This requires researchers to interface with site counseling personnel prior to the collection of interview data to ascertain procedures for referring inmates, if needed.

Finally, interviewing requires that we "ask the right questions," though at times this is a difficult task. As an example, the author offers the following account. One of the questions that was asked of all interview respondents was, "What does it mean to be a 'father?'" Typically, the respondents described what a father does, the roles that he plays, and the influence that he has, on his children. When the data collection was nearing completion, the researcher was reading the book, *Becoming Dad*, by Leon Pitts, Jr. (1999). This book details the journey to fatherhood for black men in the United States. During one of the final interviews (with a young, black father), the researcher asked the following questions:

IER: Tell me what being a father means to you.

U93: What is a father? A father is somebody that is there constantly. A father is someone who plays a part in a younger person's life. A father takes care of the home, his wife. A father is the person who sets the house on its course in terms of the morals that he got.

IER: Let me ask you this question. What does it mean to be a black father? Is there a difference?

U93: Yeah there is a great difference. Because as a black father the outside negativity and different types of influence causes that black father to shelter that child mentally because as a black father it is a double standard in society. Sometimes you might have to tell you child the reason why a race of people such as ourselves are being treated the way we are being treated is for him to understand that. You might have to tell him "you got to work twice as hard. You got to stick to it. You might not get the breaks that any other race might get." So there is much more to it. Like I explained earlier about the subliminal gestures. A lot of young black children get caught up in that. They can't really distinguish reality from what they see on television. And if the father is not wise to that then his house is in turmoil. So you got to be very keen and understanding in sheltering a young black boy.

The point here is that asking the "right" question can result in much greater detail and understanding of the phenomenon under investigation. The difficult task, of course, is "knowing" what the "right" questions are. A qualitative approach, one that combines data analysis with data collection, may offer the best opportunity for discovering the "right" questions.

IMPLICATIONS FOR FUTURE RESEARCH

The current study has presented a broad sketch of some of the concerns of jailed fathers, and the ways in which childhood experiences influence adult behavior. This study points to additional areas that deserve the attention of researchers, and these areas are outlined below.

Intergenerational Cycle of Crime and Incarceration

As reported earlier, a majority of the interview respondents had either negative interactions with, or little to no contact with their fathers. Forty percent of the interview respondents grew up absent the guiding hand of their own father and 20% reported that their father was abusive. Additionally, 20% of the interview respondents reported that a parent had been incarcerated. The extent of family disturbance was great for the interview respondents as children. Similarly, the children of these men were experiencing turmoil as a result of paternal incarceration.

While the outcomes for children who lose a parent to the criminal justice system likely vary, the potential exists for children to experience negative outcomes as a result (Johnston, 1995). Future research should examine the "Intergenerational Crime and Incarceration" model (see for example Johnston, 1995). This model suggests that when children are exposed to enduring trauma they develop "trauma-reactive behaviors" (Johnston, 1995, p. 80) which allow them to cope with difficult situations. According to Johnston (1995),

> "Without intervention, reactive behaviors become fixed patterns that help children to cope. Fixed patterns of coping behaviors may become compulsive when children have no other resources for support. Although they may initially be adaptive for highly stressed children, the compulsive coping behaviors that occur after trauma are ultimately maladaptive because they often lead to crime and incarceration" (p. 81).

While studies focusing on the children of incarcerated parents exist, most "information on prisoners' children is actually derived from surveys of their parents. Very few studies have directly examined the children themselves" (Johnston, 1995, p. 62). Another way to study this issue is by interviewing adult offenders and (perhaps a control group of non-offenders) and examining their retrospective accounts of their childhood experiences (as in the current study). This would permit for examination of the ways in which children react to trauma, and would provide information on the adult outcomes of those reactions.

Macro-Structural Influences on Parenting (and Father Absence)

Data from the interview phase of the current study imply that Black interviewees were more likely to be reared in father absent homes than were their white counterparts. Further, the interview respondents who had "absent" fathers frequently followed in their dad's footsteps. There exists in this nation a cultural stereotype of Black men as "missing fathers."[5] Chapter 2 fully outlined the ways in which macro-structural factors (e.g. joblessness, economic stress, eroding infrastructures) disproportionately impact minorities in this country. These stressors weaken the foundations of stable and long-term relationships (Wilson, 1996) so that in situations where poverty is a way of life, so too, is single parenting. Alarmingly, in 1997, 44 percent of African-American children in the U.S. were living in poverty (Current Population Survey, 1998). Further, as a nation we are spending billions of dollars on prison construction while simultaneously cutting billions of dollars for programs that would assist young Americans. These spending patterns represent a "commitment by our nation to plan for social failure" (Donzinger, 1996, p. 29).

The problem with the cultural stereotype mentioned above is that "Race" (often understood as biology) has become the proxy variable used to allude to these underlying macro-structural factors, leading individuals to incorrectly conclude that there must be "racial" differences in parenting. Parenting is a <u>learned</u> behavior. It is this author's strong contention that searching for "racial" differences in parenting, without acknowledging the macro-structural influences that affect the "learning" process, is a useless and dangerous undertaking. Therefore, future research should examine the extent to which structural factors influence parenting, and should further examine if our social and criminal justice policies play a role in father absence.

Parenting Program Evaluation

Earlier in this chapter the author argued for expanded implementation of parenting programs in jails. These programs should be linked to the specific needs of the population (jailed fathers), but more importantly, they should include evaluation components to allow for the determination of their effectiveness. Future research should evaluate these parenting programs to determine if such programs influence

---

[5] Leon Pitts, Jr. (1999), provides an excellent examination of this topic in his book, *Becoming Dad*.

paternal attitudes and behaviors both during incarceration and after release.

LIMITATIONS

This research project represents an exploratory/descriptive examination of an understudied population – jailed fathers. The study was conducted in two jails in the Commonwealth of Pennsylvania and utilized availability sampling. Consequently, the data are not generalizable to other populations. The respondents in the current study were serving relatively short sentences and thus, the current findings reflect the concerns of individuals who are measuring separation from their children in months, rather than years.

As outlined in Chapter 3, the researcher (for safety reasons) was granted access to only four pods at the large, urban jail. The inmates on these pods were low security risks. The most common offense category among respondents was drug offenses (see Chapter IV). Because of the classification system used in the urban jail, violent offenders were, for the most part, excluded from this study. The exclusion of violent offenders limited the findings of the study.

Finally, there were very few (n = 10) respondents from the small, rural jail. This study did not intend to make "urban-rural" comparisons, but future research may. If these comparisons were a focus, it would be imperative to broaden the sampling scheme to include multiple rural sites, as populations in these facilities are relatively small.

CONCLUSIONS

Data from this exploratory study present an image of jailed fathers that simultaneously supports and refutes the stereotypical "incarcerated father." In many regards, the jail is just a microcosm of our society, with both "good" and "bad" fathers represented. The "bad" fathers typically resided apart from the children prior to their incarceration, and interacted with them rarely. Their proclamations that fathers were important people were not matched by their behaviors in fulfilling this role. Conversely, the "good" fathers were involved and loving parents who spent time with their children and ached as a result of their separation. The thing both groups had in common was the mechanism by which their paternal behavior was acquired – it was learned. The current study provides a glimpse of how important fathers are, lending support for attachment theory.

Many of the interview respondents were reared in chaotic family situations where father absence, incarceration and abuse were commonplace. The negative impacts of these experiences were visible in the accounts given. The children of these respondents are now experiencing similar situations, leading to a continuation of an unfortunate cycle and placing them at risk for similar outcomes. Our jail and prison populations in the year 2010 will include children, who today, are 10 year olds.

This project represents the first study known to examine jailed fathers. While the findings from this exploratory study cannot be generalized to other populations, the data suggest significant areas for additional inquiry. The data further suggest that the implementation of family maintenance programs is critical. Failure to do so will seal the fate of tomorrow's jail population, as eloquently expressed by a respondent:

R05: As far as I'm concerned, it's a matter of common sense. It's strictly common sense. I'm here for one reason. I'm here to be punished. My kids aren't to be punished. I'm here to be punished. So why do my children need to suffer? Is it the legal system trying to get me locked up, punish me on the left hand? On the right hand my kids are being punished. The legal system knows my kids are being punished but, hey, that's job security for them 20 years down the road. They're going to psychologically harm my children 20 years down the road and my kids going to commit a violent act. Now they can put him in jail. Job security. Is that what it is? Or do they, is just that they've overlooked everything? They're so ignorant to it that it doesn't matter. It's common sense. It's a matter of common sense.

References

Adler, J. (1997, Spring Summer). It's a wise father who knows... *Newsweek (Special Edition: Your child)*, 73.

Arrendell, T. (1995). *Fathers and divorce*. Thousand Oaks, CA: SAGE Publications, Inc.

Babbie, E. (1989). *The practice of social research (5th ed.)*. Belmont, CA: Wadsworth Publishing Company.

Bakker, L., Morris, B. and Janus, L. (1978). Hidden victims of crime. *Social Work, 23*, pp. 143-148.

Bayse, D.J., Algid, S.A., and Van Wyk, P.H. (1991, July). Family life education: An effective tool for prisoner rehabilitation. *Family relations, 40*, pp. 254-257.

Beck, A., Gilliard, D., Greenfeld, L., Harlow, C., Hester, T., Jankowski, L., Snell, T., & Stephan, J. (1993). *Survey of state prison inmates, 1991* (NCJ-136949). Washington, D.C.: Bureau of Justice Statistics.

Beck, A. (2000). *Prison and jail inmates at mid-year 1999* (NCJ – 181643). Washington, D.C.: Bureau of Justice Statistics.

Benson, L. (1968). *Fatherhood: A sociological perspective*. New York, NY: Random House.

Biller, H. (1981). Father absence, divorce, and personality development. In, M. Lamb (Ed.), *The role of the father in child development* (2nd ed.)(pp.489-552). New York, NY: John Wiley & Sons, Inc.

Bleyer, N. (1995). *1994 county statistical report.* Camp Hill, PA: Office of Planning, Research and Statistics, Pennsylvania Department of Corrections.

Bloom-Feshbach, J. (1981). Historical perspectives on the father's role. In, M. Lamb (Ed.), *The role of the father in child development* (2nd ed.)(pp.71-112). New York, NY: John Wiley & Sons, Inc.

Bloom, B. and Stinehart, D. (1993). *Why punish the children: A reappraisal of the children of incarcerated mothers in America.* San Francisco, CA: National Council on Crime and Delinquency.

Bohm, R. (Ed.) (1991). *The death penalty in America: Current research.* Cincinnati, OH: Anderson Publishing Company.

Bonner, R. and Rich, A. (1990). Psychosocial vulnerability, life stress, and suicide ideation in a jail population: A cross-validation study. *Suicide and life threatening behavior, 20,* 3, pp. 213-224.

Bonner, R. and Rich, A. (1992). Cognitive vulnerability and hopelessness among correctional inmates: A state of mind model. *Journal of offender rehabilitation, 17,* 3/4, pp. 113-121.

Bonczar, T. and Beck, A. (1997). *Lifetime likelihood of going to state or federal prison* (NCJ-160092). Washington, D.C.: Bureau of Justice Statistics.

Bowlby, J. (1952). *Maternal care and mental health.* Switzerland: World Health Organization.

Bowlby, J. (1969). *Attachment.* New York, NY: Basic Books.

Bowlby, J. (1988). *A secure base.* New York, NY: Basic Books.

Bretherton, I. (1991). The roots and growing points of attachment theory. In, C. Parkes, J. Stevenson-Hinde, and P. Marris (Eds.), *Attachment across the life cycle* (pp. 9-32). New York, NY: Routledge.

Bronstein, P. (1988). Father-child interaction: Implications for gender role socialization. In, P. Bronstein and C. Cowan (Eds.), *Fatherhood today: Men's changing role in the family* (pp. 107-124). New York, NY: John Wiley and Sons, Inc.

Bryson, K. (1997). *My daddy takes care of me! Fathers as care providers* (P70-59). Washington, D.C.: U.S. Census Bureau.

Bryson, K. and Casper, L. (1998). *Household and family characteristics: March 1997* (P20-509). Washington, D.C.: U.S. Census Bureau.

Baunach, P. (1985). *Mothers in prison*. New Brunswick, NJ: Transaction, Inc.

Carlson, B. and Cervera, N. (1992). *Inmates and their wives: Incarceration and family life*. Westport, CT: Greenwood Press.

Chira, S. (1993, September,22). Census data show rise in child care by fathers. *The New York Times*, p. A-20.

Chiricos, T. (1998). The media, moral panics and the politics of crime control. In, G. Cole & M. Gertz (Eds.), *The Criminal Justice System: Politics and policies* (7th ed.)(pp. 58-75). Belmont, CA: Wadsworth Publishing Company.

Cobean, S. and Power, P. (1978). The role of the family in the rehabilitation of the offender. *International journal of offender therapy and comparative criminology, 22*, pp. 29-38.

Cohen, S., Kesslar, R., and Gordon, L. (Eds.) (1995). *Measuring stress: a guide for health and social scientist*. New York: Oxford University Press.

Cripe, C. (1997). *Legal aspects of corrections management.* Gaithersburg, MD: Aspen Publishers, Inc.

Crumley, F. and Blumenthal, R. (1973). Children's reactions to temporary loss of the father. *American Journal of Psychiatry, 130*, pp. 778-782.

Dalley, L. (1997). *Montana's imprisoned mothers and their children: A case study on separation, reunification and legal issues.* Unpublished doctoral dissertation, Indiana University of Pennsylvania.

Donzinger, S. (Ed.). (1996). *The real war on crime: The report of the National Criminal Justice Commission.* New York, NY: Harper Collins Publishers, Inc.

Edna McConnell Clark Foundation. (April, 1993). *Americans behind bars.* New York, NY.

Family and Corrections Network. (1995, June). *Parenting programs for prisoners.* (Issue 5). Palmyra, VA: Author.

Fishman, L. (1990). *Women at the wall: A study of prisoners' wives doing time on the outside.* Albany, NY: State University of New York Press.

Friedman, S. and Esselstyn, T. (1965). *The adjustment of children of jail inmates. Federal probation, 29*, pp. 55-59.

Fritsch, T. and Burkhead, J. (1982). Behavioral reactions of children to parental absences due to imprisonment. *Family Relations, 30*, pp. 83-88.

Furstenberg Jr., F. (1995). Fathering in the inner city: Paternal participation and public policy. In, Marsiglio, W. (Ed.), *Fatherhood: Contemporary theory, research, and social policy* (pp. 119-147). Thousand Oaks, CA: Sage.

Gabel, K. and Johnston, D. (1995). Incarcerated parents. In, K. Gabel and D. Johnston, MD (Eds.), *Children of incarcerated parents* (pp .3-20). New York, NY: Lexington Books.

Gabel, S. (1992). Behavioral problems in sons of incarcerated or otherwise absent fathers: The issue of separation. *Family Process, 31,* pp. 303-314.

Gibbs, JJ. (1982). The first cut is the deepest: Psychological breakdown and survival in the detention setting. In, R. Johnson and H. Toch (Eds.), *The pains of imprisonment* (pp. 97-114). Prospect Heights, IL: Waveland Press, Inc.

Gibbs, JJ. (1986). When donkeys fly: A zen perspective on dealing with mentally disturbed jail inmates. In, D. Kalinich and J. Klofas (Eds.), *Sneaking inmates down the alley: Problems and prospects in jail management* (pp. 149-166). Springfield, IL: Charles C. Thomas.

Gibbs, JJ. (1987). Symptoms of psychopathology among jail prisoners: The effects of exposure to the jail environment. *Criminal justice and behavior, 14, 3,* pp. 288-310.

Gibbs, JJ. (1991). Environmental congruence and symptoms of psychopathology: A further exploration of the effects of exposure to the jail environment. *Criminal justice and behavior, 18, 3,* pp. 351-374.

Gibbs, JJ. (1992) Jailing and stress. In, *Mosaic of despair: Human breakdowns in prison* (Rev.ed.). Washington, D.C.: American Psychological Association.

Gibbs, JJ. and Hanrahan, K. (1993). Safety demand and supply: An alternative to fear of crime. *Justice quarterly, 10,* pp. 369-394.

Giever, D. (1997). Jails. In, J. Pollock (Ed.), *Prisons: Today and tomorrow.* Gaithersburg, MD: Aspen Publishing, Inc.

Gilliard, D. (1999). *Prison and jail inmates at midyear 1998* (NCJ-173414). Washington, D.C.: Bureau of Justice Statistics.

Gilligan, J. (1997). *Violence: Reflections on a national epidemic.* New York, NY: Vintage Books.

Glueck, S. and Glueck, E. (1950).   *Unraveling juvenile delinquency.* New York, NY: Commonwealth Fund.

Goffman, E. (1961). *Asylums: Essays on the social situation of mental patients and other inmates.* Garden City, NY: Anchor Books, Doubleday and Company.

Gottfredson, M. and Hirschi, T. (1990). *A general theory of crime.* Stanford, CA: Stanford University Press.

Guttmann, J. (1993) *Divorce in psychosocial perspective Theory and research.* Hillsdale, NJ: Lawrence Erlbaum Associates, Publishers.

Hale, D. (1987).   The impact of mother's incarceration on the family system: Research and recommendations. *Marriage and Family Review, 12,* pp. 143-154.

Hairston, C.F. (1989).   Men in prison: Family characteristics and parenting views. *Journal of offender counseling, services and rehabilitation, 14,* pp. 23-30.

Hairston, C.F. (1995). Fathers in prison. In, K. Gabel and D. Johnston, MD (Eds.), *Children of incarcerated parents* (pp.31-40). New York, NY: Lexington Books.

Hairston, C.F. (1998).   The forgotten parent: Understanding the forces that influence incarcerated fathers' relationships with their children. *Child Welfare, LXXVII,* 5, pp. 617-638.

Hanrahan, K., Martin, J., Springer, G., Cox, S. and Gido, R. (1996, March). *Prisoners and separation from family.* Paper presented at the Academy of Criminal Justice Sciences, Las Vegas.

Harlow, C. (1998). *Profile of jail inmates 1996.* (NCJ-164620). Washington, D.C.: Bureau of Justice Statistics.

Harrison, K. (1997). Parental training for incarcerated fathers: Effects on attitudes, self-esteem, and children's perceptions. *The journal of social psychology, 137*, pp. 588-593.

Henriques, Z. (1982). *Imprisoned mothers and their children.* Washington, DC: University of America.

Hetherington, E. (1972). Effects of father absence on personality development in adolescent daughters. *Developmental Psychology, 7, 3*, pp. 313-326.

Hetherington, E., Bridges, M. and Insabella, G. (1998). What matters? What does not? Five perspectives on the association between marital transitions and children's adjustment. In, E. Junn and C. Boyatzis (Eds.), *Child growth and development 99/00* (pp. 139-155).

Hinde, R. and Stevenson-Hinde, J. (1991). Perspectives on attachment. In, C. Parkes, J. Stevenson-Hinde, and P. Marris (Eds.), *Attachment across the life cycle* (pp. 52-65). New York, NY: Routledge.

Houston, J. (1985). *Motivation.* New York, NY: Macmillan Publishing Company.

Irwin, J. (1985). *The jail.* Berkeley, CA: University of California Press.

Jacobs, J. (Ed.). (1986). *Divorce and fatherhood: The struggle for paternal identity.* (Clinical insights monograph). Washington, D.C.: American Psychiatric Press.

Johnson, R. (1998). *Death work: A study of the modern execution process.* Belmont, CA: Wadsworth Publishing Company.

Johnson, R. and Toch, H. (Eds.). (1982). *The pains of imprisonment.* Prospect Heights, IL: Waveland Press, Inc.

Johnston, D. (1995). Effects of parental incarceration. In, K. Gabel and D. Johnston, MD (Eds.), *Children of incarcerated parents* (pp.59-88). New York, NY: Lexington Books.

Kampfer, C. (1995). Post-traumatic stress reactions in children of imprisoned mothers. In, K. Gabel and D. Johnston, MD (Eds.), *Children of incarcerated parents* (pp.89-100). New York, NY: Lexington Books.

King, A.E (1993). The impact of incarceration on African American families: Implications for practice. *Families in society: The journal of contemporary human services, 71*, pp. 145-153.

Koban, L. (1983). Parents in prison: A comparative analysis of the effects of incarceration on the families of men and women. *Research in law, deviance, and social control, 5*, pp. 171-183.

Lamb, M. (1978). *Social and personality development.* New York, NY: Holt, Rinehart and Winston.

Lamb, M. (1981). Fathers and child development: An integrative overview. In, M. Lamb (Ed.), *The role of the father in child development* (2nd ed.)(pp.1-70). New York, NY: John Wiley & Sons, Inc.

Lanier, C. (1993). Affective states of fathers in prison. *Justice Quarterly, 10*, pp. 49-65.

Lanier, C. (1991). Dimensions of father-child interaction in a New York state prison population. *Journal of Offender Rehabilitation, 16*, pp. 27-42.

Lindquist, C. and Lindquist, C. (1997). Gender differences in distress: Mental health consequences of environmental stress among jail inmates. *Behavioral sciences and the law, 15*, pp. 503-527.

Main, M. (1991). Metacognitive knowledge, metacognitve monitoring, and singular (coherent) vs. multiple (incoherent) model of attachment: findings and directions for future research. In, C. Parkes, J. Stevenson-Hinde, and P. Marris (Eds.), *Attachment across the life cycle* (pp. 127-159). New York, NY: Routledge.

Main, M. and Weston, D. (1981). Quality of attachment to mother and to father: related to conflict behavioour and the readiness for establishing new relationships'. *Child development, 52*, pp. 932-940.

Marsiglio, W. (Ed.).(1995). *Fatherhood: Contemporary theory, research, and social policy*. Thousand Oaks, CA: Sage.

Martin, J., Hanrahan, K., Gido, R., and Moloney, L. (1995, March). *Separation, parenting, and male inmates: A preliminary report*. Paper presented at Academy of Criminal Justice Sciences, Boston.

McCracken, G. (1988). *The long interview* (Sage University Paper Series on Qualitative Research Methods, Vol. 13). Beverly Hills, CA: Sage.

McGowan, B. and Blumenthal, K. (1978). *Why punish the children?: A study of children of women prisoners*. Hackensack, NJ: National Council on Crime and Delinquency.

Messner, S. and Rosenfeld, R. (1994). *Crime and the American Dream*. Belmont, CA: Wadsworth Publishing Company.

Morris, P. (1965). *Prisoners and their families*. New York, NY: Hart Publishing Company, Inc.

Mosley, J. and Thompson, E. (1995). Fathering behavior and child outcomes: The role of race and poverty. In, Marsiglio, W. (Ed.), *Fatherhood: Contemporary theory, research, and social policy* (pp. 149-165). Thousand Oaks, CA: Sage.

Mumola, C. (2000). *Incarcerated parents and their children* (NCJ –182335). Washington, D.C.: Bureau of Justice Statistics.

Munro, J. (1976). Towards a theory of criminal justice administration: A general systems perspective. In, J. Munro (Ed.), *Classes, conflict, and control: Studies in criminal justice management.* Cincinnati, OH: Anderson Publishing Company.

Nunnally, J. (1967). *Psychometric theory.* New York: McGraw-Hill.

Palmer, J. (1985). *Constitutional rights of prisoners* (3rd ed). Cincinnati, OH: Anderson Publishing Company.

Parish, T. (1980). The relationship between factors associated with father loss and individual's level of moral judgment. *Adolescence, 15,* 59, pp. 535-541.

Pitts, Jr., L. (1999). *Becoming dad: Black men and the journey to fatherhood.* Marietta, GA: Longstreet, Inc.

Pollock-Byrne, J. (1992). Women in prison: Why are their numbers increasing? In, P. Benekos & A. Merlo (Eds.), *Corrections: Dilemmas and directions* (pp. 79-95). Anderson Publishing Company.

Quinn, R., Faerman, S., Thompson, M. and McGrath, M. (1990). *Becoming a master manager.* New York, NY: John Wiley and sons.

Ransom, R. (1993). *Doing time together: An exploratory study of incarcerated fathers and their kids.* Unpublished doctoral dissertation, The American University, Washington, DC.

Rokach, A. (1998). Loneliness and psychotherapy. *Psychology: A journal of human behavior. 35,* 3-4, pp. 2-18.

Rokach, A. and Cripps, J. (1999). Incarcerated men and the perceived sources of their loneliness. *International journal of offender therapy and comparative criminology, 43,* 1, pp. 78-89.

Roman, M. and Haddad, W. (1978). *The disposable parent: The case for joint custody.* New York, NY: Holt, Rinehart and Winston.

Sampson, R. J. and Laub, J. H. (1994). Urban poverty and the family context of delinquency: A new look at structure and process in a single study. *Child development, 65,* pp. 523-540.

Santrock, J. (1975). Father absence, perceived maternal behavior, and moral development in boys. *Child Development, 46*, pp. 753-757.

Schwartz, M. and Weintraub, J. (1974). The prisoner's wife: A study in crisis. *Federal probation, 38,* pp. 20-26.

Shaver, P. and Brennan, K. (1991). Measures of depression and loneliness. In, J. Robinson, P. Shaver, and L. Wrightsman (Eds.), *Measures of personality and social psychological attitudes: Vol. 1. Measures of social psychological attitudes series* (pp. 195-290). New York, NY: Academic Press, Inc.

Snell, T. (1995). *Correctional populations in the United States, 1993.* (Report No. NCJ-156241). Washington, D.C.: Bureau of Justice Statistics.

Sturges, J. (1998). *Social interactions between visitors and correctional officers at two county jails.* Unpublished manuscript, Indiana University of Pennsylvania.

Swan, A. (1981). *Families of black prisoners: Survival and progress.* Boston, MA: G.K. Hill.

Sykes, G. (1958). *The society of captives: A study of a maximum security prison.* Princeton, NJ: Princeton University Press.

Tasch, R. (1952). The role of the father in the family. *Journal of experimental education, 20*, pp. 319-361.

Toch, H. (1992). *Mosaic of despair: Human breakdowns in prison* Rev.ed.). Washington, D.C.: American Psychological Association.

Walker, S. (1989). *Sense and nonsense about crime: A policy guide* (2nd ed.). Belmont, CA: Brooks/Cole Publishing Company.

Watkins, K. (1987). *Parent-child attachment: A guide to research.* New York, NY: Garland Publishing, Inc.

Welch, M. (1994). Jail overcrowding: Social sanitation and the warehousing of the urban underclass. In, A. Roberts (Ed.), *Critical issues in crime and justice* (pp. 251-276). Thousand Oaks, CA: Sage.

Wilson, J. and Herrnstein, P. (1985). *Crime and human nature.* New York, NY: Simon and Shuster.

Wilson, W. J. (1996). *When work disappears: The world of the urban poor.* New York, NY: Alfred A. Knopf, Inc.

Yogman, M., Cooley, J., and Kindlon, D. (1988). Fathers, infants and toddlers: A developing relationship. In, P. Bronstein and C. Cowan (Eds.), *Fatherhood today: Men's changing role in the family* (pp. 53-65). New York, NY: John Wiley and Sons, Inc.

Index